Love Punch

Love Punch

& Other Collected Columns

Rob Hiaasen

Collected by Maria Hiaasen
Foreword by Kevin Cowherd

Apprentice
House Press
Loyola University Maryland

FOREWORD

On a chilly winter evening six years ago, my great friend Rob Hiaasen and I sat in an Irish bar in the northern Baltimore suburbs, swilling pints of Guinness.

The band was playing a god-awful Pogues cover, one that, were it ever played in the presence of Shane MacGowan, would cause the band's legendary front man to weep and stab himself with a sharp object.

Rob quickly tired of the caterwauling on stage. So we moved to a quieter spot in the back of the room, where he was eager to share news about his latest exercise regimen.

Months earlier, he explained, he'd bought boxing gloves, an 80-pound Everlast heavy bag and a speed bag. Now, every night after work, he was punching the bags for 12 three-minute "rounds" and resting for a minute between each one—just like in a real boxing match.

"I'm in pretty decent shape," he said. "In fact, I'm thinking of getting in the ring against someone. What do you think?"

I stared at him.

My God, was this the Guinness talking already!?

The man was 54 years old! I pictured him taking a shot to the jaw and—mouthpiece or no mouthpiece—watching two or three loosened teeth float through the air like gleaming Chiclets. I envisioned him taking an uppercut to the gut that would leave him crumpled and wheezing on the canvas.

"Are you out of your freaking mind?" I said finally.

"But I'm ready," he said.

"No," I said, "you're not." Not at that age, buddy.

He looked down at his beer. For an instant, his shoulders seemed to sag. Then he threw his head back and laughed uproariously.

The full absurdity of it all had finally dawned on him: a gentle sub-urban husband and dad, a Norwegian pacifist with an AARP card—a man whose last dustup with another human being had occurred when he was 12 and another kid punched him in a middle-school gym for allegedly breaking his love beads—climbing into the ring against some skilled brute half his age, with a lump of scar-tissue for a face.

And all for *exercise*, no less!

Yet even as Rob's pipe dream faded in the din of the noisy room and the conversation turned to other topics, I knew one thing was cer-tain: he'd get a column, one way or another, out of this boxing fantasy.

And just days later, he did.

In fact, it's re-printed right here ("Love punch"), in this wonderful collection of columns he wrote for the Annapolis *Capital Gazette* from 2010 until last year, when an unspeakable shooting at the newspaper claimed his life and the lives of four of his colleagues.

Also included is a short first-person piece Rob wrote for *The Baltimore Sun*, where he worked as a gifted features writer for 15 years. It's about a damp, nervous evening he spent as a chaperone for a middle school dance. You can almost feel the hormones bouncing off the cafeteria walls in his re-telling.

Like the man himself, the columns in this book are often big-hearted, whimsical and self-deprecating. They're keenly-observed slices of everyday life—to my mind the very best gift a general columnist can give his or her readers.

Many, like the pieces that chronicle Rob's love for dogs, his iffy luck with cars and his wariness of modern technology, will make you laugh out loud. Some, like the touching "What I Did On Spring Vacation," about visiting the grave of a long-dead childhood friend and pulling weeds from the simple marker, might even make you misty-eyed.

More than anything, what these columns represent is a fervid appreciation for life—and of the common humanity in all of us.

Whether kindly mentoring young reporters as an editor at the *Capital Gazette*, wandering the bustling streets of Annapolis and his beloved

Eastport neighborhood looking for column ideas, or teaching the next generation of journalists as an adjunct professor at the University of Maryland, Rob constantly strove to connect with others and learn what makes them tick.

He does that again throughout this delightful collection, where his love of story-telling shines through on every page.

Kevin Cowherd
Cockeysville, Md.
February, 2019

[1]

Newsies

Don't pass (expletive deleted) notes

March 16, 2014

I sympathize with the mayor. Wow. I've never uttered those words about a politician. But I do sympathize.

This past week, a frustrated Annapolis Mayor Mike P. passed a note to an alderman during a prickly public discussion.

"Thanks for (expletive deleted) me," the mayor's note read.

Mike P. apparently then made private amends to offended parties. But the note had already made headlines. It was embarrassing. It was dumb. It was interesting. And it was human.

Still, there's a lesson here—a lesson I failed to learn.

When I was in the fifth grade I had a girlfriend named Jean M. Our relationship existed primarily—if not exclusively—on paper in the form of passed notes. That I had her house on constant weekend surveillance neither enhanced nor threatened our bond. The point was I had her in my sights.

But the course of true love seldom runs smooth, as they say.

I don't remember what was so alluring about Diane S. Maybe it was the way she walked to the chalkboard or sipped her chocolate milk. Maybe it was the way she absolutely ignored me—yes, that probably was the way. Whatever the attraction, I felt compelled to start writing her notes. Surely, she could read; hadn't we all begun working together on reading in kindergarten?

I don't remember the contents of my first and only note to Diane S. My guilt remains an open case (Jean M. hovers to this day on Facebook) since I'm pretty sure I threw her under the school bus. No doubt, I sloppily professed my affection for Diane S—while not mentioning any home surveillance I might have had in mind. Upon reading my words, her heart would have no choice. Soon, Diane S. would be sharing her chocolate milk with Rob H.

But our love was intercepted.

It wasn't an alderman, citizen or alert reporter who exposed my note that spring day. It was my elementary school nemesis: Bill M. Foolishly, I had asked him to hand Diane S. my note. She was just two rows over, after all. But that scoundrel, in between stabs of satanic laughter, read my letter out loud. He always did have a good speaking voice, I'll give him that.

To Jean M.'s surprise, to Diane S.'s disinterest and to my horror, my note went viral in a musty classroom of Peters Elementary. Had there been Google, I would have crashed the operation or landed a book deal.

My remaining days of fifth grade were spent largely alone. Writing notes to girls or stalking their homes didn't feel as rewarding anymore. But because few of us stop while we're behind, I resumed my note passing in the sixth grade.

Diane M.

Yes, another Diane.

Another bad idea.

Dear mayor, allow my story to be a cautionary tale. Let's keep our notes to ourselves no matter how honest, stupid, human and regrettable they may be. Because there will always be a Bill H. setting us straight and on other courses in life's better passing.

Sine Die Another Day

April 13, 2014

The General Assembly's 2014 legislative session concluded this past week with all the hoopla and excitement of, well, watching laws being made.

But who can blame lawmakers? They can't have hot, hot, hot button topics every year. How often can you bust out the Dream Act, gun-control laws and same-sex marriage? Can we blame the closing-moment confetti from looking a little bored?

I just wish lawmakers could have mustered the moral and political courage to pass legislation that affects me.

Don't get me wrong. I'm not in favor of revenge porn, holding 10 grams of pot, knocking back grain alcohol, and driving while texting—and especially not at the same time. But not one of my personal bills passed.

For example, I supported a bill that would physically move the state of Maryland next to my home town of Ft. Lauderdale because I still really like the beach there. The measure never got out of committee. The measure never got out of head. Consensus-building is not my strength, and it hurt me this session, too.

Take my proposed legislation to regulate motorists wishing to make a left on West Street when I'm behind them and oncoming traffic suggests multiple electrical poles have just toppled onto West Street. Is the Dunkin' Donuts really that good to hold me up like this?

This was another defeat. You know how the state bird is the Western Meadowlark? I proposed the state bird be changed to the Meadowlark Lemon—my favorite Harlem Globetrotter who brought me more joy than any bird. I again failed to secure a co-sponsor—and a parking spot anywhere near the State House. How does the state of Maryland expect me to get involved in government if I can't park?

My hallmark legislation, if passed, would have eliminated vehicle emission testing, vehicle registration, vehicle parking, vehicle tax and tags, and common vehicle obstructions such as tolls, inexplicable lane closures and Forest Drive. But in a stinging critique, the Maryland Department of Legislative Services labeled my proposal "fiscally criminal" and recommended a special session be called to consider a restraining order against me.

The experience taught me a valuable lesson. Politics is indeed a contact sport—unlike ping-pong, which I proposed become the official state sport. But the powerful pro-checkers lobby foiled me. And not Chinese checkers but good ol' U.S.A. checkers.

I had other proposed legislation that never got a fair hearing. The last day of the General Assembly is traditionally called *Sine Die*, which is Latin for "Not the Best Headline." My bill would have changed *Sine Die* to *Sine Die Another Day*. Opponents were quick to criticize my James Bond reference, calling it "sophomoric" and "not even close to being the best Bond movie."

Finally, I proposed a maximum wage increase to be directly deposited into my checking account.

This, too, failed.

Listen, I'm no politician. I'm just a guy who dreams of a more perfect democracy centered on my needs.

Sine Die Another Day, my fellow citizens, *sine die.*

Behind closed doors

May 4, 2014

Once again our Republic's inalienable right to petition the government misses the mark.

In Maryland, a petition drive is underway to prevent a bill to prohibit discrimination based on gender identity. The "Fairness For All Marylanders Act" has been labeled by opponents "the bathroom bill" for fear, in part, that men will be able to walk right into women's restrooms.

But the true weakness of the petition is that it fails to address the more serious issue of discrimination—the unjust and glaring disparity in quality between men's rooms and women's rooms.

Consider your run-of-the-mill public men's room. What are its defining features?

Allow me to paint a picture.

You enter the men's room of your favorite dive bar. The door does not lock much less close all the way. Graffiti papers every square inch of the cubicle; Death Row cells are bigger. You think you recognize one phone number on the wall, but it's just a bad dream.

To enhance the je ne sais quoi, some men's rooms still feature a coin-operated condom machine that hasn't been used since 1972 judging by the retro brands. There is no door to the lone stall because it was ripped off by a disgruntled patron using only his teeth.

There is a stained sink. The hand towel dispenser is strictly theoretical. There is running water if one relaxes the molecular definition of water as one part oxygen, two parts hydrogen atoms. Men's room water is missing something chemical upstairs, if you know what I mean.

In short, the men's room is the type of environment best experienced in a hazmat suit. If you don't own one (why would you?), don't touch anything. And whatever you do, don't linger. If you do linger (why would you?), you risk leaving with a tattoo or a yet-named infection.

Allow me to paint another picture.

Watch your step—there's a couch there. Sorry, a *chaise lounge*. The cushions, red velvet.

Would you care for some sparkling water with a twist of lemon? No? How about a glass of Sauvignon Blanc? We offer a nice Kim Crawford that's not too citrusy but maintains a hint of passion fruit.

You've noticed the chandelier. It's French. The gold-plated faucets, Corian countertops and individually-lighted vanity mirrors were put in a few years ago. The artwork was upgraded—some ladies thought the Pollock too explosive and unsettling, so we toned the walls down with Wyeth and Hopper.

If you're still waiting, please consider our complimentary chai honey sticks, steaming hand-rolled towels and our small library in the anteroom. The new-age music you are enjoying—"Mating Whales: The Greatest Hits"—is specifically chosen for your complete relaxation.

You've probably also noticed we have replaced those tacky cans of Glade with a working herb garden. Feel free to pinch off some fresh mint for your sparkling water or for our "Thank God It's Mojito Friday!" events held in the restroom's library.

Two restrooms—two very different pictures.

Isn't it time we end this foul discrimination?

Please join me then as I launch a petition drive to get the "Equality for All Restrooms Act" on the ballot in November. Because our children and our children's children should live in a world where all restrooms are equal.

Now, hand me some mint.

My brain on pot

March 2, 2014

Normally I don't take positions on issues because that requires thinking about issues, and frankly my time is better spent binge watching "House of Cards."

But given the General Assembly is weighing several pot bills, I feel compelled to speak out.

I urge Maryland lawmakers not to legalize or decriminalize marijuana, which, as we know, leads to massive deaths. But that's not why I oppose pot.

They say it takes 1.2 million muscles to frown but only four muscles to smile. Some of us are proud of our 1.2 million muscles. My fear is that pot will insidiously attack that muscle group and before I know it, I'll be smiling, which, as we know, leads to relaxation.

And relaxation leads to happiness, which leads to living longer, which leads to more thinking, which leads to more thinking about issues, which leads to frowning, which leads to unhappiness.

To illustrate this tragic cycle, let me tell you a story about a Baby Boomer who smoked pot three times (I'll wait until that preposterously low number sinks in). Each incident was more harrowing, more frightening than the next:

Early 1983:

Under the cloak of Daylight Saving time, the Baby Boomer secures pot (quality and origin unknown) from a supplier resembling one of those Duck Dynasty dudes. The transaction is a nervous affair. The young man grossly overpays for he is certain he'll be captured by the FBI and shipped to a Turkish prison where cable TV is spotty at best.

Safely locked in his apartment bathroom, the young man attempts to roll his first joint. The work does not go well. For sealing purposes, he considers using Krazy Glue before remembering this, too, is a gateway drug and will only compound his Turkish prison sentence.

Somehow, a joint is fashioned. He lights the twisty end. He attempts a puff. The puffing does not go well. He tries again until he finally inhales. He is smoking pot. Alone. In front of his bathroom mirror. It is not relaxing.

Later to friends, he likens the sensation to inhaling bottom-dwelling food scraps found in any kitchen disposal.

Middle 1983:

He has someone ("a friend") pay for the pot to avoid even a hint of extradition to a foreign prison. His friend proves to be a talented buyer, roller and puffer.

Safely locked in the same Orlando apartment, both young men smoke pot. As Led Zeppelin's "Whole Lotta Love" shreds their eardrums, a Monopoly board materializes. It is brought out to the pool, where both of them commence a game of floating Monopoly aboard leaky beach rafts. Hilarity ensues over the yellow property "Marvin Gardens." The name is the funniest thing ever said or heard. They call each other Marvin for the remainder of the experience.

They judge the time as either 2 in the morning or 2 in the afternoon.

It's a very relaxing time.

Late 1983:

In his last brush with the demon weed, the Baby Boomer finds himself in possession of pre-rolled and pre-paid "marijuana cigarettes." This time, he fears no Turkish prison. It is an extremely relaxing evening—until a new fear emerges.

What happens if he likes relaxing too much? And then what happens if one day Marvin Gardens isn't hilarious anymore?

It hurts the brain to think that much.

How to enjoy your shutdown

October 6, 2013

On the bright side—OK, there is no bright side, but just stay with me here—the thousands of Americans affected by the government shutdown have something the rest of us can only dream of.

Free time!

Am I being insensitive? Mean? Me? Impossible. I'm just trolling for some levity.

The challenge for me would be to fill my free time with productive, life-affirming activities. So, as a dubious public service, I offer 10 Things To Do While Furloughed:

More time for hobbies! Remember all those pet projects you wanted to get to around the house but pesky work kept getting in the way? Now you have time! So, go ahead and retreat into your man cave and work on that dartboard you've been pining for lately. You know, the one with the likenesses of Congressional leaders on it.

More time for family! Thanks to the shutdown, you can spend more quality time with your family! And how many of us long to work less so we can spend more time with our loved ones?

More time for family! No, seriously, I'm asking. How many?

More time for career planning! What better time to look for another job than when you have been inhumanely shut out of your current job and your spirits have been harpooned? Time now to polish your resume and track down references in hopes they still walk among the living. (One tip: your references might also be furloughed, so you might want to take it easy on the shutdown humor.)

More time for exercise! No more using employment and that "feeding my family" excuse for not losing those hideous 15 extra pounds. Time now to go to the gym every day! Sweat, shower and stare at people you don't know!

Every day.

More time to write personal letters! No, wait, that was for the shutdown in 1976.

More time for quality TV viewing! "Breaking Bad" is over, but take the time to reconnect with other great television drama. Of course I'm speaking of "River Monsters: Unhooked."

More time for reading! No more gobbling down your favorite book or newspaper while gobbling down your lunch or dinner. Turn being furloughed into a golden reading opportunity! Finally, here's your chance to tackle "Moby-Dick" and shave 10 years off your life! Finally, here's your chance to leisurely savor your favorite hometown newspaper—whatever publication I may be referring to.

More time to travel! What better time to spend money on travel than when you don't know when or if another paycheck is coming! Imagine hours of complete relaxation lounging on a beach in Bermuda and the only care you have in the world is running out of rum, followed closely by bankruptcy.

More time to give to others! Let's face it: employment keeps us all from doing things for free. But here's a chance to volunteer at a soup kitchen, become a Big Brother or Sister, volunteer to be a riverkeeper or get involved in politics. Because, as we were taught, we all can make a difference in Washington!

My, what powerful average-sized hands you have

March 13, 2016

Spoiler alert: I will not be voting for Donald Trump in Maryland's primary on April 26. This will not be a set-back for his campaign.

As you know, Maryland's anti-climatic presidential primary comes relatively late in the primary season, an election customarily marked by not a single in-state candidate sighting.

I could be wrong this year.

Donald Trump could hold a rally on deck of a skipjack at City Dock or drop by the *Capital Gazette* editorial board for a chat. I'd like to see that. I'd like to see his hands.

Before last Thursday night's mannered debate, Trump and remote rival Marco Rubio had discussed hand size at an earlier GOP debate. Rubio un-joked about Trump's alleged tiny hands. "You know what they say about men with small hands...," Rubio teased. Trump un-joked that his hands were more than fine—powerful things, in fact. "I guarantee you, there's no problem," he assured a worried nation.

Trump's Denver Broncos-like defense of his manhood aroused news cycle after cycle of commentary. My favorite spin-off was the Portland man who legally created a political action committee called "Trump has Tiny Hands." I discovered this gem on the same website where I was treated to "Haunting Photos of the World's Most Evil Men as Children." No mention of *their* hands.

You do know what they say about men with small hands?

Blink twice if you do.

Once if you don't.

I see a lot of double blinking out there. Whew. Because I don't want have to stoop to explain the link between impersonal hand size to personal appendage size—a slander, I should add, that was started years ago by a tribe of mean boys with very big hands. Far it be for the national discourse this presidential year to stoop even lower to talk about this subject one syllable more. I'm certainly not going to stoop that low.

However, I noticed a few of you blinking just once.

Journalists, no matter the delicate nature of the subject, must also represent the single-blinkers in our Republic. They, too, deserve to be informed by a free, average-sized press.

First, we need to separate myth from fact.

Myth: Hand size is a reliable indicator of the size of a man's you-know.

Fact: Hand size is irrelevant. But due to advancements in the dubious yet entertaining field of juvenile comparative anatomy, other factors do have scientific correlations.

The following factor are proven indicators:

- Length of inseam: Abe Lincoln had quite the inseam, just saying.
- Length of work commute: You know what they say about a man with a long commute, he's got one helluva long—commute.
- Length of back hair: (I know this isn't pleasant to hear, but we're all adults.) Say you're at the beach and you see a man with a forest growing on his back, your first reaction is one of fear and repulsion. This is understandable. But just know he's got a fun night planned.

The point is if Rubio really wanted to gain ground and hit Trump below his Trump-designer belt, he would have questioned the front runner's inseam, commute or back hair.

Not to stoop too low or anything.

Politics and cats don't mix

April 27, 2017

I don't write about politics because—and this gets delicate—I hate politics.

No, it's not that I hate politics. It's just that I don't like talking about it. Growing up, our family never talked about politics, religion, money and never, ever about sex. The one time that subject came up was when a stray cat strayed into our backyard and, I guess through immaculate conception, had baby cats. When I broached the subject, talk turned swiftly to whether our Miami Dolphins could go undefeated for the entire 1973 season.

When I was young, I asked my dad how much money he made. He looked at me like I had asked him to forward his salary to the church of Scientology. I changed the subject back to the Dolphins.

As a card-carrying journalist of 35 years, I often have politics coming out of my ears (which is embarrassing to clean up in public). I can't imagine readers needing one more journalist to tell them what they think or should be thinking or doing. Between the late night hosts and cable news and comedy shows and political websites and what's that other thing? Wait, yes, and between all those *newspaper*s, too, who needs another political expert, commentator, talk show host or columnist?

Still, when a man uses bullet items, he can't resist sharing his political musings and advice:

The border wall

No matter how you feel about bordering us off from Mexico at incalculable costs, instead let's consider a trip to our neighborhood Lowe's. They got all kinds of fences and pretty cheap. If, as a country, we opt against a Canterbury or Victorian garden fence, we can pick up a white, vinyl "Privacy Fence." Not only is it made in the U.S.A. (whew!), but we could paint it red and blue, too.

Don't know what 2,000 miles of decorative privacy fence will set us back, but say goodbye to all those illegal perennials sneaking over the border.

North Korea

This is a toughie. That dude is scary nuts.

Be smart.

National monuments

The president signed an executive order that could lead to the reduction or elimination of some national monuments. The 1906 Antiquities Act gives presidents the power to limit use of public land for historic, cultural, scientific or other reasons. Decisions made by recent presidents to preserve such lands are now under review.

But what about those '73 Dolphins??!!

Syria

Another toughie. Complicated. Sad.

Be smart.

Climate change

Future winter in Annapolis, a crisp 88 degrees ... I went snorkeling with a friend at the artificial reef that was once the Market House. Afterward, we waded over to watch Navy Seals train at the Naval Academy, which locals have taken to calling the found city of Atlantis. My friend's snorkel mask was leaking, so we gave up and got into my kayak.

As we rode the quaint yet vigorous currents up Main Street, our thoughts turned to the scientific reality of man-made global warming. After a thoughtful 30-second discussion, we broke out our fishing tackle and cast for rockfish above what we think was the old Subway. Caught our limit before finding dry land in Crofton.

Mexico

Big. Neighbor. Undocumented perennials.

Be smart.

Tax reform

The president unveiled a tax cut proposal that would apply a 15 percent business tax rate not only to corporations but to small businesses. The standard deduction for individuals would increase, reportedly providing a modest cut for middle-income people.

As I said, I don't like talking about money.

But what about that cat??!!

[2]
It's That Time
of Year

Dispatches from the dawn of 2015

January 11, 2015

Presently, the thermostat in my house is set on *Perish*.

Keeping the thermostat sub-humanely low saves money and energy. It also erases the uncomfortable contrast normal homeowners experience between a house with power and a house without due to a storm, or whatever. In my house in winter, it always feels like the power is out.

I must be saving a lot of dough and energy, which are fine, upstanding goals.

Still, one is alarmed when the family Labrador—a breed genetically crafted for frigid temps—himself dons one of my old fleece jackets from Land's End. He's trying to tell us something. He's trying to tell us that, unless we can compromise on ye olde thermostat, we have mere weeks to live.

I'm not going to say thermostat wars are a gender thing, but I am going to say thermostat wars are a gender thing.

The weaker sex ("males") are generally more ursine and carry more body weight and hot air in general. One would think we wouldn't mind it a little frosty in the home. Not so. We want lots of heat to sweat even more.

The stronger sex ("females") are generally more feline and carry less body weight and wear socks to bed during heat waves. One would think they need it toasty in winter. Not so. I don't know why.

All the others ("others") must look at us and wonder, how do the sexes survive especially in winter?

We don't want to scuffle with Delaware because we were taught never to pick on someone smaller than us. And by "we," I do mean "we"—just in case Delaware grew a lot last year and can now beat me up.

But the new year brought news of Delaware's first tourism branding campaign. The news caught our attention because Delaware isn't known for embarking on marketing adventures. When you're tagged "The First State," where do you go from there?

Turns out the folks who run Delaware (a Native American word meaning, roughly, "He Who Does Not Stop While Passing Through to Manhattan, which was Kind of Stolen from Us") got to studying their state's image. Essentially, what they found was their image can be broken down into two germane categories:

1. Bland image.
2. No image.

So, they've come up with the slogan "Delaware: Endless Discoveries"—and they're not talking about 1-95 tolls. Apparently, there's endless things to see and do in Delaware. Who knew?

Me, I'd hit the Bethany Beach angle hard.

I'm not an Ocean City guy. I'm a Bethany Beach guy, always have been. And try as I might and do, I can't *will* Bethany Beach to be in Maryland. Sure, I pretend I'm still in Maryland when I visit Bethany.

But Delaware rightfully claims Bethany Beach, which is an endless discovery in itself and which *should* be in Maryland.

It's estimated some 45 percent of people who join a gym in January quit by February.

Finally, there's help for these people.

Introducing the imaginary gym!

Just imagine shedding those unsightly holiday pounds in a matter of imaginary months. Imagine what your imaginary friends will say! *Am I imagining things or does he look 20 years younger?*

Here's what you get with your annual imaginary gym membership:

Imaginary treadmills, free weights, weight machines, ellipticals, recumbent stationary bikes.

Sound mentally exhausting?

You bet.

But if you sign up today, you will also receive imaginary very attractive people in Under Armour working out next to you. During our open enrollment period, these imaginary very attractive people will compliment you on how you look 20 years younger.

So, why be one of the 45 percent who quit real gyms in abject shame? Join an imaginary gym and just imagine how good you'll look and feel in the new year.

Remember, "No imaginary pain—no imaginary gain!"

P.S. I just received an email from Baltimore Gas and Electric Co. encouraging customers during this cold spell to set their thermostats to 68 degrees or lower.

Don't talk to me about lower.

Talking about the Sunday scaries on Mother's Day

May 13, 2018

Sundays were born rough.

Someone called them the "Sunday scaries," which is perfect. Others just call them the Sunday blues—that diagnosis-defying, fog-like funk that comes in on tiger feet. If you know someone who is wild about Mondays, you can bet they get the Sunday scaries. Mondays are rescue missions.

So, today, another Sunday, another Mother's Day.

I can't pick up the phone to call my mother anymore. Poor, selfish me. But Sunday was our day to talk on the phone. She was in Florida; me in Maryland, as was our chronic geography.

We had this running joke on Sundays. "You must have read my mind because I was thinking of you," she would say. I'd say something back along those lines. We weren't mind-readers. We were having the Sunday scaries.

The world brims with lousy talkers and lousier listeners. My mother was neither.

Like a neutral biographer, she stowed the chapters of my life in all their messy hope. She logged my job changes, relationship changes, address changes, mood changes, hair color changes—her youngest getting gray at 28?! Well, dear, it looks good on you, she would say.

Why do fibs from mothers sound like Valentines? And because youngest children prefer the camera stay on them, I'd lament my gray-then-white hair through the decades.

If she ever got tired of my whining, she never let on. Took some nerve to complain about hair color to a woman in a wheelchair who needed help in the bathroom. Even then she listened.

I'd like to think she taught me to listen, but I have a long way to go on that front. Without her knowing, she did teach me how to ask questions. Hers were personal but somehow never prying—at least they didn't feel that way after I left home. In middle and high school, I wanted no part of her questions.

Because of her, I came to believe the only questions worth asking are personal. What a gift for someone to lay low in silence just to hear your answer. It's how people begin to trust one another. It's how people fall in love, you know. Might be how we stay in love.

If you're lucky, you don't wait too *damn* long to grow up and appreciate your parents. (She would not have used damn and would have questioned my use of it. So, in her honor, a redo.)

If you're lucky, you don't wait too long to grow up and appreciate your parents.

So, she and I talked on the phone Sundays about personal things. As the years ticked off, our conversations dwindled. Then what happened—along with every awful thing that happens with an aging parent—is our talks ended. Too tiring, too much, too hard by the end.

Before that, though, in all those years of talking and listening on those scary Sundays, she was there.

In our make-believe meeting of the minds, I would call, and she would know exactly when I'd be calling. I'd wait to hear that opening invitation, that most personal of questions:

"How are you, son?"

'Momisms'—The A List

May 10, 2015

We asked around the room here at *The Capital* for any "Momisms"—sayings, advice, directives popularized on the home front by Moms.

You know what we mean—chestnut chants that are embedded in our DNA only to be passed on to unsuspecting generations. There are regional, cultural and generational differences among Momisms, but the spirit sure feels universal.

Here are a few favorites:

"Put on a shirt for dinner."

"Hate is such a strong word."

"You are going to sit there until you eat those brussels sprouts."

"Kill them with kindness."

"Did you get enough to eat?"

"Blow your nose, you'll get more out of it." (In response to people blowing the car horn.)

"You're using up all the hot water."

"Bless your heart."

"Stop it. You're gorgeous."

"If you sneeze twice, it means you'll be receiving a letter in the mail." (Actually, this is a fact.)

"If you don't have something nice to say, then don't say it."

"Worrying isn't going to change anything."

"You can't always get what you want" (with this Mom donning Mick Jagger accent)

"What Lola wants Lola gets."

"I brought you into this world and I can take you out."

"Be yourself."

First Person: The Old Man and the Sea

May 12, 2013

For many of us, Mother's Day is a time to reflect on all the unsung work fathers do with little thought to their needs, allergies and nap schedule. Hence, Mother's Day is the ideal Father's Day, and, as we know, the word "hence" doesn't kid around.

It's probably too late to return the Mother's Day card and gift, so go ahead and hand it over to her. But it's also not too late to plan your special Father's Day gift.

Take a moment today to ask: what does your father deserve? Of course, he deserves many things, but pick just one. And none of these homemade cards or gifts. None of this spending quality time together, either.

Think material things. Think wonderfully expensive material things.

Think boat.

You know he wants one. You've seen him watching all those fishing shows—Deadliest Catch, Deadliest Tuna, Deadliest River Monster, Deadliest Perch. You saw his list of dream boat names—*Comp Time, Second Mortgage, Bankruptcy II.* Do you remember that night you caught him on his computer scanning 4,000 listings on Boat Trader? Remember how fast he shut down his computer after you busted him?

"A father isn't a father until he has owned a boat." Hemingway said that. Not Ernest, just some dude named Frank Hemingway. The point is your father will never be complete until he's the captain of his ship—and can remember what day the recyclables go out.

Let me tell you a little story about a man who owned three boats, one bigger and more expensive than the next. His last boat—a 28-foot Cobalt, was harbored at Mears Marina in Eastport (now that man drives there, stands outside the locked fence, and gazes at his old empty slip—which, on the page, sounds a tad pathetic).

Many years ago in the Time Before College Tuitions, the man bought the white bow rider with a blue hull and Volvo inboard. Oh, she was yar. Oh, she hated starting. Oh, that first day at Mears, when the new boat owner did not secure her properly. Oh, the phone call two weeks later from the adjacent sailboat owner who presented an estimate of damages.

The man eventually took his boat out to sea. Above him, postcard blue Annapolis skies, and knifing around him, 52,000 sailboats, and below him, nine inches of water. Did he run aground a time or two on the mighty bay? That, he did. Did he wish he had taken a course on boating safety? He did.

But, by God, he was a boat owner—the captain of his ship and soul. Every day on the water was Freedom. Every day on the water was Father's Day. Every day at the boat mechanic's was Father's Pay Day.

You know how this story ends.

His children got older, and family boating trips became forced-marched outings. The man went out on his boat less and less. He never truly got over his fear of approaching sailboats and propeller-ending shallows. He tried fishing, but there were no river monsters or tuna. One day, he sold his 28-foot Cobalt for THOUSANDS less than he paid for it, and this from a man who NEVER uses all caps.

Man and boat weren't right for each other, or maybe their timing was just off.

So, today on Father's Day, better to give your father a funny card or some WD-40.

That's good on boats, I hear.

25

For all the boys who wouldn't grow up

May 24, 2015

"Somebody has to do something, and it's just incredibly pathetic that it has to be us."

Sometimes a person tells you something so profound, so come-to-Jesus, that you swirl it around in your brain like mouthwash.

Jerry Garcia of the Grateful Dead, who when not singing "What a long, strange trip it's been," also said, "Somebody has to do something, and it's just incredibly pathetic that it has to be us."

He was talking about (I think) stepping up to take care of our children, our communities, our earth.

He was talking about us, the kids. Us, the grown-ups. Us, the kids/grown-ups.

This past Monday the man quoting Garcia's line to the graduates of University of Baltimore's Law School was Maryland Attorney General Brian Frosh, who was not, to my knowledge, a member of the Dead (a straw poll of family members attending the graduation believed but were not positive they voted for Mr. Frosh. It was a hot day in Baltimore, so forgive their civic memories).

Brian Frosh was speaking in the context of Freddie Gray when he laid Garcia on us; we can't wait for the grown-ups to show up because, as pathetic as it may be, we're the grown-ups. Or the kids. Or both.

Many of us don't set the bar very high when it comes to graduation speakers. While their intentions and messages are sincere, the speeches make you want to scurry back into the womb and dream of a massive do-over. All this talk of finding your way, taking risk, making mistakes, learning from your mistakes, finding your passion, following your dreams, changing your dreams, changing your sheets—all that insufferable journeying, learning and changing. It was much easier being womb-based—working and living out of the home, so to speak.

But Frosh's speech kept me upright and in the real world. And there was a law professor who had the grown-up job of eulogizing a law student who died in a car accident three weeks before graduation. There are, she said, eulogy credentials and resume credentials—which are more meaningful and important? The things we say about ourselves on our resumes or things said about us in eulogies?

(Have you read your resume lately? Has there ever been a piece of writing that says so very little about you? Has there ever been a more heartless, calculated—and necessary—document created in your name and *by your own hand*? The truth, of course, is all between the lines.)

In eulogizing their classmate who couldn't be with them, this graduation speaker quoted not from Jerry Garcia but from J. M. Barrie, whose own strange trip led to "Peter Pan" and this:

"Pan, who and what art thou?" Hook cried huskily.

"I'm youth, I'm joy," Peter answered at a venture. "I'm a little bird that has broken out of the egg."

At this point, dear grown-ups, this boy almost lost it, as I was reminded again how ceremony can be so grounding, spellbinding and communal. It takes growing up a bit to see and feel this.

All this past week in Annapolis there has been ceremony in all its customary predictability and power. For it's the season of graduating, the season of man and woman, boy and girl. In the natural world, it's the season of pollen and popping azaleas, and osprey and falcon chicks breaking out of their eggs.

It's the season of eulogies and resumes, youth and joy.

And finally, this from a man who never spoke at a Maryland graduation:

The only joy in the world is to begin.

Cesare Pavese—who was also not in the Grateful Dead.

A belated Father's Day card

June 14, 2014

Thank you for assuring me I wouldn't drown when water was filling the bathtub. I was very young and very sure the water would keep coming and what would happen then?

You showed me that spot under the faucet, that little emergency drain.

Thank you for introducing me to your favorite athletes.

Joe Louis. Sugar Ray Robinson. Sam Snead. Together, we liked Joe Frazier (you were not an Ali guy) and Jack Nicklaus.

Thank you for all your music I didn't like then.

Duke Ellington. Ella Fitzgerald. Louie Armstrong. (You were not a Charlie Parker guy.)

Those old albums of yours? I have them now on CD.

Thank you for your work bench. I kept your level and some weird massive wrench. I never saw you use it. I haven't used it. But I like having a weird massive wrench in the unlikely event a major construction project bewitches me.

Thank you, thank you, for taking us to the Florida Keys all those summers. I complained because my friends were going to faraway places like Chimney Rock in a faraway land called North Carolina while we were stuck going *again* to the Keys—a whopping 2½-hour drive from our home.

I miss the Overseas Highway (off-season) bisecting the Atlantic and Florida Bay, those water colors, those roadside restaurants serving conch fritters and fresh dolphin.

I still get to the Keys when I can. I need the place.

Thank you for, on sneaky occasion, giving me the first cold blast of your Pabst.

Thank you for your love of boats.

You bought me and my brother that 12-foot Jon boat from Sears. We'd get tiny fiberglass splinters hauling it around. I taught myself how to handle a small boat in the Everglades and Key Biscayne. I learned a boat is better than any car will ever be. And our 7.5 Merc outboard was moodier than I was.

Thank you for the golf lessons. I still can handle a 9 iron, but golf didn't stick with me. Damn you, long irons.

Thank you for going to my basketball games. Watching me made you nervous (playing made *me* nervous). You didn't go to many of them. That's OK. Please know I improved my free throw shooting.

Thank you for taking me to Disney World the year after it opened. You would have much rather been on a golf course, or fishing, or listening to Louie Armstrong in your La-Z-Boy, or watching Don Shula's Miami Dolphins beat everybody. But you went to the Magic Kingdom, suffered the long lines, indulged me, fathered me.

Thank you for maybe the greatest Christmas gift. 1970? My brother left for college. You turned his bedroom into your office. This was not my idea. My idea was that his room—bigger, better—should be passed down to me. I communicated this to you on many occasions.

You didn't budge for months.

Then, that Christmas, you bugged out of the corner bedroom. You actually deeded me the room—a legal document you drew up at your law office. I became the official owner of my brother's bedroom. As it should be. I still keep the deed in a lock box just in case someone tries to steal the memory.

Over the years I've become a memory hoarder, but I wish I could remember more things to thank you for on Father's Day.

At least this year I have a card.

Music Fact: The 70s sounded better than the 80s

July 12, 2015

What was the better decade for music—the 70s or 80s?

Looking for a free summer parlor game to play with anyone, anywhere?

Try the "What decade had better music?" game.

Last weekend, I was enjoying a bit of the grape on my back deck when someone irresponsibly declared the music of the 80s better than the music from the 70s. After consulting with more of the grape, I called upon my tiger-like musical reflexes to settle the argument before it could get out of hand, i.e. me losing.

To secure victory, I announced my list of Top Ten Albums of the 1970s (with honorable mentions):

"Rumours"—Fleetwood Mac

"Born to Run"—Bruce Springsteen

"Who's Next"—The Who

"Songs in the Key of Life"—Stevie Wonder

"Sweet Baby James"—James Taylor

"Some Girls"—The Rolling Stones

"Aja"—Steely Dan

"Innervisions"—Stevie Wonder

"Goodbye Yellow Brick Road"—Elton John

"Blood on the Tracks"—Bob Dylan

Honorable mentions: "Let it Be"—The Beatles, "Chicago Transit Authority"—Chicago, "Tapestry"—Carole King, "Eat a Peach"—Allman Brothers, "Turnstiles"—Billy Joel, "Off the Wall"—Michael Jackson, "Court and Spark"—Joni Mitchell, "More Songs About Buildings and Food"—Talking Heads. (And pick any 1970s Led Zeppelin or Al Green album of your choice.)

So, what we were arguing about again? How the 1980s had better music?

Prove it. Write me; I promise to be open-minded unless it looks like I'm losing.

The bloody curtain rises on 10 great Halloween movies

October 29, 2017

Dear horror fans, let's forget about crime, politics and sports—even sports!—in this humble space so we may entertain and frighten ourselves.

Halloween is Tuesday. There's talk Gov. Larry Hogan might extend summer vacation to include Halloween, but so far the talk is coming only from me. There *has* been deadly serious talk around the newsroom about great Halloween movies. (Spoiler alert: Journalists have potent cinematic opinions when unkenneled from news gathering duties.)

We asked the crew to send top picks and a few words on why their Halloween movies are so obviously great. Italicized are the guest reviewer's comments, along with occasional yet gifted editor's notes.

So, in no order, cover your eyes:

"Psycho" (1960): *I did not use a shower for years after seeing it as a young child. Finally had to in college when someone put a log in the dorm bathtub for an art project.* Editor's note: Alfred Hitchcock used 78 camera set-ups and 52 cuts for the 3-minute shower scene. The murdering "mother" was a stand-in for Tony Perkins.

"Halloween": The 1978 original, of course. *From script to direction to cinematography to score, the scariest "slasher" movie in the genre.*

"Freaks" (1932): *Still the best last 10 minutes in any horror film ever.* Editor's note: Director Tod Browning bet everything on this twisted pup—and lost his career. Baltimore's own, the torso-less Johnny Ecks, played one of the "freaks."

"The Shining" (1980): *Rather than focus on dumb crap like jump scares, bad antagonists more memorable for their look than their motivations and poor lighting effects, Stanley Kubrick actually make you feel uncomfortable through a series of unknowns that aren't just "what's around the corner?"*

"The Nightmare Before Christmas" (1993): *For when you're inebriated post-Halloween party. Trust me.* Editor's note: We do.

"Eraserhead" (1977): *Unsettling, ominous and unnerving, this is less a horror film than it is an experiment in assailing human psyche through explicit, unexplainable and yet still humanizing imagery with little context. For a 1977 indie film by David Lynch ("Twin Peaks", "Blue Velvet"), the depiction of a mutant newborn and the (seemingly) dreamlike state Jack Nance's protagonist character navigates the world did more to upset me than any Chucky doll.*

"Night of the Living Dead" (1968): Editor's note: George Romero's cult classic (shot for $114,000) set the walking dead bar for all zombie cinema to come.

"You're Next" (2011): *This horror-slasher flick is equally scary and surprising as it turns traditional movie tropes inside out. You might think you know what's going on, but you have no idea until the very end! Great movie for people who love tense action sequences, jump scares, dark humor and copious gore.*

"Hocus Pocus" (1993): *Whether or not you grew up watching this on the Disney Channel, it's a classic. Bette Midler, Sarah Jessica Parker and Kathy Najimy are a wonderfully witchy force to be reckoned with as the Sanderson Sisters. Midler's wickedly sassy rendition of "I Put A Spell On You," and Parker's haunting "Come Little Children" have become part of the soundtrack to so many millennials' Halloweens. It's a perfect film for all ages.* Editor's note: Well said, but who are these millennials you speak of?

"House on Haunted Hill" (1959): Editor's note: When I was in middle school in 1971, this was an after-school movie in our darkened cafeteria. Vincent Price plays a Vincent Pricey-millionaire who invites five people to his haunted house and offers $10,000 to anyone who can stay the night. I vividly remember a jangling skeleton emerging from a vat of acid. I vividly remember because I dream about it still.

Guest reviewers: Chase Cook, Selene San Felice, Dan Griffin, Phil Davis, Wendi Winters and Rob Hiaasen.

American horror story

October 30, 2013

I've become that house.

You know the house.

The house on Halloween that doesn't want to play along anymore. The house on your street owned by the older parents who don't find Halloween nearly as amusing because their shuttered, dark hearts won't allow for such amusement anymore.

The house that *turns off the lights* on Halloween.

Oh, such a cruel twist.

There was a time that I, the Dark-Hearted One, raided Michaels for the latest in artsy skulls, crafty witches and jumpy skeletons. I played scary organ music from a hidden Boombox, propped up a life-sized coffin on my front stoop, and dressed as Dracula if you can imagine Dracula as the tallest, meekest suburbanite whose voice was a cross between Pee-wee Herman and Darth Vader.

I gave out *good* candy—bars and bars of it. None of this two-items-per-kid nonsense. I let all those sticky fingers dive in and pillage. Sure, I ran out of candy in 20 minutes and had to run back out to the Rite Aid. Sure, I quickly invoked a one-item-per-kid rule resulting in scattered tears. I was still Mr. Halloween.

"And what are you supposed to be?" I'd kindly ask all those young, adorable trick-or-treaters. Their answers were often precious and surprising.

But the question began to haunt me as the years bled on.

"And what are you supposed to be?" I'd kindly ask street-clothed, 17-year-old miscreants who looked like the guys I advised my daughters never to come within 50 feet of.

They did mean things to my pumpkins.

No more candy for them!

Or anyone!

For now I lurk in partial darkness, a prisoner in my home, clutching my stash of Milky Ways, mine I tell you, all mine. I close the shutters in the front so the little and big ones can't see me hiding behind my HBO, my candy wrappers mounding on my belly, and my glass of red wine for re-enforcement.

Younger parents have replaced me, and so be it. These parents, to my horror, who have their own ideas about Halloween.

This year Halloween falls on a Thursday. No problem, right? It's more of a treat to have Halloween on a school night. What's the big deal about going out on Saturday night? One of the universal laws of the universe has been and should be Halloween is celebrated Oct. 31. But now there's an effort to postpone trick-or-treating to Saturday.

On my street, I was asked to support Saturday trick-or-treating. I could not. I did not. I believe my side lost.

So come Saturday, tricksters might hear the sounds of spooky music or see broom-flying witches impaled face-first into trees or meet a neighborhood Dracula with an equally lame impersonation.

It just won't be at my house—unless I can find something awesome at Michaels. I hear Miley Cyrus costumes are hot this Halloween.

Me twerking. That ought to *really* scare the kiddies.

The Twelve Days of Christmas (Reconsidered)

December 20, 2015

On the first day of Christmas
My true love sent to me:
A Partridge in a Pear Tree.
* * *
On the second day of Christmas
My true love sent to me:
2 Turtle Doves
And a sweet but flimsy explanation why I need a partridge or a pear
  tree.
* * *
On the third day of Christmas
My true love sent to me:
3 French Hens
2 Turtle Doves—which I have no idea where to keep much less what to
  feed.
And no need for a partridge or a pear tree (grapefruit tree, sure).
* * *
On the fourth day of Christmas
My true love sent to me:
4 Calling Birds
3 French hens—is this like a solidarity thing with the French?
2 Turtle Doves—which in no way look like or are as cool as turtles.
And no need for having what will only end up as compost.
* * *
On the fifth day of Christmas
My true love sent to me:
5 Golden Rings
4 Calling Birds—do they *have* to call? Can't they sit quietly and think
  underwhelming bird thoughts?

3 French Hens—solidarity. Check.

2 Turtle Doves—not real turtles.

And no need for that first stuff we mentioned.

* * *

On the sixth day of Christmas

My true love sent to me:

6 Geese a Laying

5 Golden Rings—You didn't tap into our IRAs, did you?

4 Calling Birds—That can call from another zip code.

3 French Hens—Vive la France!

2 Turtle Doves—Vive la Dinner!

But there's no need for threatening violence against turtle doves.

* * *

On the seventh day of Christmas

My true love sent to me:

7 Swans a Swimming

6 Geese a Laying—Try: 6 Geese a Staying Away from Other Frisky Geese.

5 Golden Rings—Think one ring. Zales.

4 Calling Birds—Retired.

3 French Hens—Growing on me.

2 Turtle Doves—Bacon-wrapped, pepper-spiked, with oozing cream cheese...

And the reason for being chintzy on the rings is because it cost $1,100 to have one chintzy dead Chestnut tree chopped down lest it crush my home for the holidays.

* * *

On the eighth day of Christmas

My true love sent to me:

8 Maids a Milking

7 Swans a Swimming—Where?

6 Geese a Laying—Platonically.

5 Golden Rings—Zirconium.

4 Calling Birds—Mute.

3 French Hens—Love them!

2 Turtle Doves—With a Syrah or a nice Chardonnay.

And I'm sorry but any number of maids a milking doesn't sound like an
    appropriate gift.
* * *

On the ninth day of Christmas
I napped.
* * *

On the tenth day of Christmas
I un-napped.
* * *

On the eleventh day of Christmas
My true love gave to me:
11 Pipers Piping—No.
10 Lords a Leaping—No.
9 Ladies Dancing—Yes.
8 Maids a Milking—No.
7 Swans a Swimming—No.
6 Geese a Laying—No.
5 Golden Rings—No.
4 Calling Birds—No.
3 French Hens—Yes.
2 Turtle Doves—No.
1 Partridge in a Pear Tree—No.
* * *

On the twelfth day of Christmas
My true love gave to me:
Assorted Drummers Piping, Pipers Drumming, Lords a Milking, Ladies
    Calling, Maids a Swimming, Swans a Doving, Geese a Sneezing,
    Lord of the Rings, Very Quiet Birds, French Hens, Turtle Doves,
    and, I give up —
Throw in the partridge in a pear tree, too.

Dear Santa. I want stuff. Thank you.

December 6, 2015

How about a R2-D2 humidifier for a Stocking Stuffer?

Dear Santa,

Howdy.

My kids tease me about saying "howdy" because while I'm a Southerner, I'm not *that* much a Southerner. You're a Northerner, of course. How do you greet people at the North Pole? I'm guessing "howdy' is out of place. More of a formal "hello" kind of deal? Yes, I'm stalling because it's not my nature to jump right into asking for stuff.

I want tougher gun laws.

No, no, just kidding! I could use a new wallet. Mine is frayed. It's a serious problem. I can't expect to maintain my breakneck level of professional success with a weakened wallet.

I want an international climate deal.

Come on, fooled you again Santa! I'd really like a Mistletoe Drone. I saw one for $70 in the Hammacher Schlemmer catalog. *This is the mistletoe that imparts whimsical cheer to holiday gatherings when hovered remotely over celebrants' heads.* Imagine flying that baby at the office party! For those of you whose office parties were discontinued because of the exorbitant cost to your multi-million dollar corporate owners, fly the drone on some random Friday at work. Imagine the festive sexual harassment lawsuits!

I want peace in Baltimore.

Sorry, I'm cracking myself up here. Seriously, I want WD-40 with a Smart Straw. I ran out. This is important. (P.S. I love that straw, so please make sure my new WD-40 has one. Thank you.)

I want anyone caught poaching an elephant or enjoying recreational lion hunting to serve time at Guantanamo.

Just a little wildlife slaughter humor there! Seriously, I want an R2-D2 humidifier just in time for the new "Star Wars." *Artoo also incorporates a night light to ensure a room does not slip over to the Dark Side.* If you can throw in a Darth Vader Barbesaber for my next barbecue and maybe the Darth Vader Toaster that imprints "Star Wars" on each evil slice of bread, I promise not to ask for another thing, Santa.

I want peace in Syria.

Got you again! Who do you think I am—a holiday buzz kill? Santa, I got two words for you: plantar fasciitis. Nothing says holiday spirit more than plantar fasciitis. Peyton Manning has it. I have it (we have so much in common). Again look no further than Hammacher Schlemmer: Item #1: The Gentleman's Plantar Fasciitis Herringbone Slippers. Item #2: The Plantar Fasciitis Insoles. Item #3: The Plantar "Twister" Game—for the sore of heel and young at heart (not featured in catalog).

I want comprehensive immigration reform.

Like a hole in the head!

OK, I'll stop kidding around. Honest, I want a Charlie Brown Musical Christmas Tree authentically wrapped in Linus' blanket. With that one ornament and sad little pine tree. Because like Linus, I know the real meaning of the holidays.

The real meaning is wanting and buying stuff from catalogs.

Everyone knows that.

It's the most wonderful time of the year

December 22, 2013

"What do you want for Christmas?"

"Let's not get each other anything this year."

It's the most wonderful time of the year

With the kids jingle belling

And everyone telling you "Be of good cheer"

It's the most wonderful time of the year...

"We say this every year, and we end up getting each other something."

"Seriously, let's not buy each other anything. We have enough."

"I know, but I have an idea for you this year."

It's the hap-happiest season of all

With those holiday greetings and gay happy meetings

When friends come to call

It's the hap- happiest season of all...

"Do you know what it is?"

"I know."

"So, you don't want a Kindle? You don't think you'd use a Kindle?"

There'll be parties for hosting

Marshmellows for toasting

And caroling out in the snow

There'll be scary ghost stories

And tales of the glories of

Christmases long, long ago...

"So, no Kindle?"

"I like real books."

"Is there a book you'd like?"

It's the most wonderful time of the year

There'll be much mistletoeing

And hearts will be glowing
When love ones are near
It's the most wonderful time of the year...
"If you buy me something and I don't buy you anything, then . . ."
"Let's just not buy each other anything this year."
"You say that, but then you buy me something."
There'll be parties for hosting
Marshmellows for toasting
And caroling out in the snow
There'll be scary ghost stories
And tales of the glories of
Christmases long, long ago...
"What are you looking at on your comp?"
"Would you wear a button-down sweater?"
"I'm not sure what that is."
"A sweater that's not a pullover."
"Oh."
It's the most wonderful time of the year
There'll be much mistletoeing
And hearts will be glowing
When love ones are near...
"I'm not sure I'm a button-down sweater kind of guy."
"So, what do you want for Christmas?"
"I don't know. I thought we weren't getting each other anything?"
It's the most wonderful time...
"What about a Tablet? Would you use a Tablet?"
"That's something I'd need to pick out."
It's the most wonderful time...
"What are we going to get the kids?"
"I don't know."
"Money, I guess."
"We could get them a few little things like we always do."
"And money."

It's the most wonderful time...
"What about your mother?"
"I don't know."
It's the most wonderful time...
"What about your mother?"
It's the most wonderful time of the year
"So, are we going to get each other something this year?"

One smokin' hot Christmas

December 27, 2016

Editor's note: This column was reprinted from 2013. There have been no further reindeer incidents.

Christmas is a time of sharing—and not just food or gifts, but also profound, timeless memories.

My family had a Styrofoam Santa sleigh with a plump cotton Santa and nine wax reindeer. The decoration was a family heirloom, which isn't remotely true but the heirloom angle punches up the story.

The heirloom normally was set out by the Christmas tree in the living room. When I was 11 or so, I got to keep it in my bedroom. I remember lifting it up and pretending Santa was flying through the air. The sleigh had little pretend presents glued to it. And there were those nine wax reindeer.

Two nights before Christmas, I asked my best friend to come over. It was urgent, I told him. But when I showed him the Santa sleigh, he was not overjoyed or even joyed. He was hoping I had discovered a stash of *Playboys*, which would have explained the land speed record he broke running to my house. When he saw it was just a Styrofoam Santa, his Christmas spirit was broken, and I felt foolish.

Maybe it was the lack of quality adult magazines, I don't know, but I had one of those ideas so profoundly stupid it made future mistakes seem like child's play.

I lit the family heirloom on fire.

You have questions, I know. What is a kid doing with matches? Where were his parents? Why did he want to burn down Santa of all people? Did he eventually receive the psychiatric help he obviously needed?

Hey, I wasn't trying to burn down Santa. I liked the old guy—believed in him, you could say. I just wondered what would happen if I lit the tip of a wax reindeer antler. Just the tip.

Shockingly soon, flames. I had never witnessed a fire—especially one in my bedroom. Steve and I watched in odd awe, as Santa's entire operation went up in smoke. Untested in the ways of fire, we became alarmed when the curtains caught fire.

I opened the window to let the smoke out, as Steve quietly went to the bathroom in the hall. He shuttled Dixie cups of water into the burning bedroom. We discovered Dixie cups are not optimal fire-fighting equipment. So, we formed a brigade and managed to douse the festive inferno. One wall had smoke damage, so I pulled an NFL poster off the other wall to cover it (thank you again Joe Namath).

After a cooling-off period, I stowed the charred sleigh and reindeer nubs under my bed. Santa himself survived intact, probably due to a flame-retardant material long since outlawed. Sensing the night's fun had concluded, my best friend went home. The fire, if nothing else, had taken our minds off any phantom Playboys.

Alone, I had a choice:

1. Tell my parents about torching a favorite Christmas decoration and risk not getting a Spalding football from Santa.

2. Don't tell my parents.

I chose the latter for reasons best explained in No. 1.

But this Christmas season I decided to break my silence in hopes of preventing others from making the same mistakes.

Don't mess with fire, kids.

And don't ever, ever, mess with Santa.

A symbol up in flames

January 30, 2015

The story ritual is terribly familiar:
An all-consuming hell fire.
Missing people. Children, included.
Statements from surviving family members.
Statements from the school.
Media stake-outs. Front pages. Internet headlines.
Teddy bear memorials.
Rumors.
Cordoned search for remains.
Body found. Another. Six.
Then, the cause of the hell fire.
Faulty electrical outlet.
Accidental.
The instrument of the fire? Its unwitting carrier?
A Christmas tree.

A warm symbol of the most joyous, decorated and family-knit occasion for many families—a tree-skirted, star-topped ritual signifying tradition, charity, family, Christ, peace on earth.

A Christmas tree.

But won't we worry more about them now? Will we remember to water it enough? Are the needles starting to look a little dry? Won't we assign someone in our families to turn off the tree before the last one goes to sleep?

Won't some of us make sure we unplug the tree every night?

All those little lights, all that big electricity.

We'll watch it like a hawk.

And when the holiday has worn off, we'll get a little down to see our tree stripped of its family ornaments and knotted light strings and drying out before our eyes.

It was a good tree, we'll say.

We'll remember yet another Christmas.

And how wonderful to be grandparents and having the kids over to see the tree. Knowing you bought them stuff their parents probably didn't want them to have, but you don't have to play by any gift rules.

If you want to keep the tree up way past Christmas, that's your call, too. What's the rush? Why not keep the tree up a little longer for them?

Why not keep the tree up a little longer for *you?*

There are the folks who take down their tree the day after Christmas, the folks who wait a few days, maybe a week, and there's those who just keep delaying.

Why?

Because it's harder for some to take it down, to let go for another year until we start the ritual again of...

Picking out a Christmas tree.

Let's get a big one this year.

Maybe just have white lights and red ornaments. Do something different for a change.

Or we can do the same as we do every year because it's our Christmas tree.

And it will be a good one, we'll say.

Lost money found after holiday plea

December 12, 2014—updated from previous publication on December 10, 2014.

Update: On Wednesday, someone claimed the $500 turned in to Annapolis police earlier this week. "It does sound like a happy ending," said Marla Weisenberg, who had found the money and turned it in.

After offering a helping hand, she needs one.

Marla Weisenberg of Annapolis was taking a late walk downtown Monday night with her dog and not much on her mind other than let's make the walk quick. It was cold and drizzly, so hurry up your business.

As she walked along Franklin Street near the Banneker-Douglass Museum, something on the ground caught her eye.

Money.

"Kind of a lot of money," she says.

The kind of a lot of money you don't want to leave on any ground. What to do, what to do.

It's not common for that much money to be lying around the streets of Annapolis. Could be stolen—or not.

Weisenberg took the money home and the next day she made the rounds around Church Circle, dropping into the courthouse and post office and anywhere to leave word about what she had found. When no one had any leads, she turned the envelope into Annapolis police Tuesday afternoon. Talked to a nice officer, she says. Got his business card and a case number and everything.

"I just want them to have their money back," Weisenberg says. "I don't want them throwing up their hands thinking their money is just gone."

So, the search is on for "them"—or he or she or, maybe, them. Someone missing a kind of lot of money around the holidays.

Marla Weisenberg won't talk about how much or any other details because she wants to leave that to the police to handle the claiming end of things. She just wants the money back where it belongs.

"To make their Christmas a little merrier," as she says.

If anyone has a clue about the case of the missing money, call Annapolis police at 410-268-9000 and ask for Officer Rodney Butler. He's a nice man, we hear.

[3]

Of Boys and Men

Were you talking to yourself again?

May 28, 2017

As I was saying to myself, "You talk to yourself too much. It's disturbing. And you're starting to scare others."

I was loping around outside and having a riveting conversation with myself when I nearly trampled a fellow traveler. She was clearly a high-end professional type given her dress, height, poise and "I shall sue you now" vibe. Talking to yourself is far easier than talking to others, as we all know. But talking to someone else about the fact you were just caught talking to yourself is some tough talk.

Our exchange:

Me: "I'm sorry. I was talking to myself and didn't see where I was going."

Her:

Me: (Still hoping for a response and a way to avoid being subpoenaed, I put on a little something called "The Charm." It's too nuanced and bewitching to articulate, so just stand back and enjoy.)

Me:

Her:

Me:

Her:

As I walked away, I asked myself out loud if other people talk to themselves and if so, is there a special section in heaven for us self-talkers? While thoroughly researching stories about people who talk to themselves, this headline popped up first: "It doesn't mean you're crazy—talking to yourself has cognitive benefits, study finds." Bingo.

A study published in *Quarterly Journal of Experimental Psychology* (you have a subscription, right?) says most people talk to themselves at least every few days, and many report talking to themselves on an hourly basis. So-called self-directed speech in children can help guide behavior and sharpen their thinking chops.

And for adults?

Cognitive benefits were also found, the study said. In one experiment, 20 people were given the name of a supermarket item. In the first trials, the participants couldn't say a word to themselves or anyone. In the second set, they repeated the object's name out loud. According to the findings, the latter crew found their milk or cheese or whatever much easier in the store than did the silent shoppers.

Having learned I'm not crazy but rather one smart shopper, no further research was necessary.

A day later, I ventured out of my work environment to lope about in the comfy 92-degree heat. I had many discussions with myself, some of which centered on my next trip to Wegmans and what I might require for a weekend of successful eating. My clinically-approved, self-talking led me through a parking lot, across one median and what might have been someone's back yard. As I circled back to *our* parking lot, I met another fellow traveler.

Me: "Sorry about that. I was talking to myself again." (Tip: when caught talking to yourself, look sheepish and charming; i.e., a charming sheep.)

Her: (Laughing) "That's OK. I do it all the time."

Me: "You do?"

Her: "Sure. Everybody does."

I smiled. She smiled. We walked on.

When it dawned on me: The trick, all those fallow romantic years ago, wasn't talking *to* girls, it was talking to myself while nearly trampling them.

So, dear single readers, keep on talking to yourselves. You never know who you might trample.

First Person: For my first trick, a hobby

March 24, 2013

The question will come. Maybe not tomorrow or the next day, but it will come. And it's a question so hurtful, vile and unmerciful that only friends dare ask it.

"So, what'd you do this weekend?"

I will be seized by rapid memory loss. I will stall for time. My concession speech will be three words.

"I don't remember."

Later, I do remember. I did laundry, loaded the dishwasher with my signature cramming, and watched re-runs of "Pawn Stars" because Chumlee is the greatest. On Sunday I dealt with my sock drawer, where I unearthed an old cigar cutter. I don't smoke cigars, but maybe I should.

I need manly hobbies to tell anyone daring to pry into my understated lifestyle.

"My weekend? The usual. I finished my ballroom dancing lessons on Saturday morning. In the afternoon, I whittled an armoire for the little lady, who requested I cease and desist whittling and calling her "little lady." Sunday morning, I opened a chain of quality soup kitchens, rebuilt a '58 Chevy engine (it wasn't my Chevy but the puzzled guy's next door). Later, while renovating the second bathroom, I accidentally spackled the dog. We had a good laugh over that, as we smoked cigars and played chess. My dog is lousy at chess, but he cuts a mean cigar."

Somewhere there's a healthy, fulfilling medium on the Male Hobby Spectrum.

Somewhere.

As of Spring 2013, my list of perceptible hobbies features:
- Checking the doors at night to see if they're locked.
- SDM: Seasonal Disorder Moping.
- Trespassing in a nearby cornfield with my dog Earle, where he chases low-flying Canada Geese (unlike people, dogs know

when to give up the chase), and where he eats deer hooves.

Deer-munching—now that's a manly hobby. Why don't I roam tilled cornfields and forage for downed mammals? Imagine the savings from never eating out again. Oh, but I can hear the naysayers: Man is not meant to devour festering, raw deer hooves.

Which leads me to a site called "The Art of Manliness," which lists 45 more traditional hobbies for my consideration:

3. *Ham radio* (and its less popular sister hobby, Head Cheese radio).

4. *Wood working.* "When you're taking a chisel to a piece of wood, it's easy to enter a zen-like state" or a zen-like emergency room.

5. *Reading.* I've heard of this.

6. *Backpacking.* No, no.

7. *Cooking.* (See: *Backpacking.*)

8. *Fly fishing.* I know a lot of men fly fish and wade in lovely streams and wear long-sleeved, pricey clothes and tie flies. (How do they get the little fellas to sit still?) But fly fishing seems like a little something I like to call "work."

9. *Paintball.* I don't know what this means.

10. *Magic.* "Every man," the site says, "should know at least a couple of good magic tricks to impress friends, woo ladies, and delight children."

For my first trick, I will make the dishwasher load itself, as I roam cornfields and never give up the chase.

When the water hits the fan

April 6, 2014

I keep in my head and in notebooks a rag-tag team of sayings that have kept me company over the years—words from friends, actors, poets, licensed plumbers.

"Young men should travel, if but to amuse themselves."

"Humor is just anger in a pretty dress."

"Relationships are never over—they're just over *there.*"

There's another saying, which will define my April.

"Water wins."

My basement flooded last week, and I'm sticking to this story:

Spring, that liar, told me to turn on the outside faucets so I may soon water all the dead stuff in my yard. In my basement, I reached up into the dropped ceiling whereby I was showered by insect remains. Shaken, I still managed to turn on the valve that allows water to flow to the outdoor faucet.

A day or two later—let's say three days—I descended into my basement. It smelled like an overturned ark—or old feet. Apparently, a rare indoor typhoon had hit the room—or a frozen pipe burst (I'm no expert, so I can't definitively rule out a typhoon).

Among the damaged goods: drywall, ceiling, carpet, treadmill, my soul, a framed movie poster of "Young Frankenstein," sofas, chairs and a T-shirt I left down there circa 2011.

Because I'm slow to process bad news, I pondered the situation for a week. In the interim, the damage did not cure itself. I had to take action, which in my line of DNA, is easier said that acted.

I made a few calls, which promptly set into motion a stage of life anthropologists have long since called "The Coming of Men Into the Home." Usually in the morning they came. In large colorful trucks these water mitigators came. I lead them to the basement and got the hell out of their way.

I've never experienced dehumidifier envy before, but buddy, I got it now. After gutting and ripping and slashing out property parts, the water mitigator men placed three magnificent dehumidifiers on the bare floor. They took aim at whatever was soaked and exposed because although water does win, one must still put up a fight.

The best part was the Dexter-like plastic sheet (with a cool blue zipper) they used to cordon the chunk of ruined basement. It's been the first thing I do when I get home: I scamper to the basement, open the zipper, stick my head in the room, and stare at the dehumidifiers. I don't know at what point a quirk becomes a troubling hobby, but I'm closing in.

For five days, the water mitigator men have come to my home. I hear them unzip the sheet, and I wonder what *they* see when they look into the dead room.

After five visits, I'm told their time is up. They will visit one final time to remove the magnificent dehumidifiers and cool blue zipper. Soon, other men with financial ties to basement flooding will come to the home. But they won't be the water mitigator men.

You never know who you'll miss, do you?

And darkness fell upon us

November 3, 2013

And there came upon the land a period of darkness, and the darkness had a name—the Red Sox Nation—and we entered this darkness against our will but with strength of heart and conviction.

And today there came upon the land additional darkness, and the darkness also had a name—the Time of Lost Daylight—and we entered this darkness also against our will but with equal strength and conviction.

Certain men have always dreaded the Time of Lost Daylight—the darkened commute, the deprivation of one hour of sun-fed life, the sudden, psychotic temper tantrum because the TV remote needs Triple AAA batteries and there aren't any in that cramped kitchen drawer but there are, for some sick reason, three unopened packs of Double AA batteries no one living will ever need.

These strong, wonderful men aren't alone.

For in our land millions of such people suffer from that which is named seasonal affective disorder—or what our elders less clinically referred to as "being a Mr. Cranky Pants."

In the Time Before—the Time of Daylight Saving ... (I know, you want to say Daylight *Savings*, which sounds like the friendliest bank ever, but the term is Daylight *Saving*, and I've managed to bore myself with this, too) ... these people lived energetic, in-the-ballpark happy lives. They were able to change the batteries in the TV remote without medication or how ever many free counseling sessions their health plan offered in the Time Before HealthCare.gov.

These same men, so pathologically Scandinavian, took daily nourishment from the saved daylight. They were communicative. Their faces could contort into actual human expression. They were productive at work. They changed the air filters at home. On the sunniest of days, they even waved to neighbors.

But starting today, in the Time of Lost Daylight, these men will again become susceptible to mood swings ranging from A to B. In the coming months, it will only get worse. They will develop a blood-thirsty craving for carbs. Their musical tastes will turn violently to the blues. Smiling will require a medical procedure. Family members will bear witness in early February—around the Time of Another @#$% Birthday—when the sun will show itself for three hours a day and when Mr. Cranky Pants needs to move out.

For Mr. Cranky Pants will be felt and heard around the house and hearth (but moreso around the house for one is unsure of what a hearth is). In this Darkest of Time, he might even raise his voice. Yes, we said raise his voice.

And in this Time of the Raised Voice, he will soon thereafter take refuge under his covers for an extended period of sleep not to exceed early-to-mid April—or what our elders referred to as Spring Training.

The season of renewal. The season of light.

The Season of the Orioles.

The book of us

May 25, 2014

I started the first book of us in 1988.

I was going to be a father for the first time and wanted to write my son a letter. So, I wrote him a long letter six months before his arrival. Because I'm a writer by nature, my nature had more ambitious plans. I started a journal.

Here were my rules:

1. Write whatever I want.
2. Write whenever I want.
3. Show no one.
4. Finish when I finish.
5. Give the journal to him on the day of his college graduation.

The journal took seven years, then I put it in a safety deposit box—actually, one of those lock box things. Stowed it high on a closet shelf. Several times I peeked to see what I had written. There were major gaps in time. Major world events omitted. Family occasions skipped.

What I recorded were the tiny flashes within a young family—first words said, fifth words said, beginning toys, beginning interests, the dog I rescued and then put up for adoption because it was the wrong time to have a dog. Mainly, I wrote about my son, my wonderful boy in all his boyhood. I also wrote about myself—too much so, I know now.

Because time stampedes us all, I found myself 22 years later handing him the freed journal at his college graduation dinner. The weight of the journal in my hand, the weight of these specks of memory, buckled me. But if a father can't cry at a crowded restaurant, then where can he? The privacy of his garage? Did that, too.

I forgot Rule No. 6:

6. The day you finish the journal, start the next one.

And I did.

It took me about six years to write the second book of us. If I could do simple math on the spot, I'll tell you how old my daughter was when I started her journal (around 5, I think). I filled her journal with photos of her playing soccer and dressed for Halloween as a puffy pumpkin, sweet scribbles she wrote me on my birthday, a column I had written about my kids. Again, my writing was sporadic but steady.

Two years ago, at a different restaurant but for the same milestone, I gave my daughter her journal. I again had released it from its fault atop my closet. I again peeked and read snatches of dinner table conversation, a play-by-play of a vacation somewhere, a dog that stayed, some job change of mine, a brother who sometimes teased her, my utter hopes for her. The tears again came over our nice dinner.

Rule No. 6:

6. The day you finish the journal, start the next one.

And I did.

In October 2001, I started the third book of us—to my second daughter and last child. It took me about five years. The journal was a different style than the other two—it had little pocket folders. I tucked an old business card in there, artsy notes she wrote me for no reason, a crazy photo of her catching a bluegill at arm's-length. Much talk of our two dogs then, Bethany Beach then, our universe *then*.

Then, this past Monday, my daughter graduated from an art college. We had a celebratory dinner. But I saved the moment until we got back home where I gave her the third book of us.

I read from the first page. *This is for my talented girl who is going to be an artist one day*, I wrote 13 years ago. And the artist and her father cried, but not at a restaurant this time.

Talking about a dream job at the University of Maryland

October 21, 2017

This past week I was in the company of young people. You know the type.

Young.

People.

And they were all over the place at a career fair for the University of Maryland's Philip Merrill College of Journalism.

There was an intern recruiting task at hand but like the best of us, my mind wandered to that distant land the brochures call Memory. For not only was I in the company of young people, I was in the company of their youthful eagerness, earnestness, shyness, boldness, handshakes and resumes.

A few words about resumes in 2017.

These artful platters of accomplishments give us older types Freudian levels of resume envy. Although it does warm the heart to know students still stick to one page, their resumes devour the white space leaving a take-no-prisoners transcript. After reading one stellar resume after another, they meld into one skyscraper of heaping accomplishment. At the rate some of them are going, they will have had 56 jobs by retirement. One of which will be your boss.

This is neither the time nor place to discuss my college resume by way of comparison. Today's college students, however, do not have the hardships I faced (girls, beer, free concerts on the lawn, Burrito Brothers, Frisbee). Like I said, there's no need to elaborate here.

Now about today's handshakes.

Some border on acts of violence; you could press charges for the gripping assault you just experienced. We get it: You're young and strong. Calm down, hand. And because this hasn't changed either, there still exists what I call the mystery handshake. This requires you to suspend the fact you *know* you're shaking a human hand and allow yourself to entertain harrowing possibilities. Why, I must be shaking an athletic sock I found wedged behind the drier. Or, am I shaking a poor limp creature my dog excavated from the backyard?

Mostly I encountered quality handshakes—but there is room for improvement, young people.

There is something surreal (if not subversively comical) about finding yourself the adult on the other side of the table. All these young faces looking at you as if you know something they don't. When it's time to open your mouth you say things believing you know something they don't. Five hours later you get in your car and ask yourself, "What in the hell was I yammering about?"

Maybe something stuck, maybe something you said was worth the parking garage fee. Honestly, probably not.

Then you remember what someone told *you* when you weren't yammering. It sprang from a question you asked after crippling fatigue set in as it invariably does when given a grown-up chore. Don't you remember? You asked that one college kid:

"So, what is your dream?"

And without hesitation and without consulting his resume, he said, most earnestly and eagerly:

"I want to be a great dad."

You wanted to but you couldn't reach across the table and hug the kid or the career fair police would have revoked your parking and handshaking privileges.

But talk about a dream job.

Over a barrel

September 29, 2013

I hope you have started to read our week-long bay series, which began today online and on our front page. The series makes me think about what I can do to help.

Buy a rain barrel, Hiaasen, you slacker.

These common store-bought barrels capture stormwater runoff, which is a leading contributor to the bay's sickness and stories I edit at *The Capital.* Many folks and businesses have them. But I don't, despite the facts: my home features a roof, the roof gets rained on, and the rainwater leads to the bay because every inch of the mid-Atlantic leads to the bay.

My weekends lead to Home Depot, so while I was there last Sunday I went barrel hunting. Once inside my orange palace, I hung a left, stopped to leer at the Weber gas grills, then entered the kingdom of the garden center.

"Do you have rain barrels?"

"What?"

"You know, rain barrels."

The man consulted with another man, who, after relaying the Ravens-Texans score, led me to the barrels.

Because I want some things in life to be simple, they never are. Before me in the Twilight Zone Aisle was something called a Basketweave Urn with built-in planter. I hadn't planned to do any planting whilst saving the bay, but it's good to know I can. With typical deliberation, I took 25 seconds before buying a $113, 60-gallon, rainwater collection system with built-in planter.

At home, I propped the urn up next to a drain spout by the garage door. I had identified this location as the primary source of all bay pollution since 1608 when John Smith first landed on my property. Next, I unfolded the handy installation guide. I imagined a speedy setup, then back to the Ravens game—or should I say back to the Redskins game for those far less fortunate fans.

Not to brag, but I *am* pretty handy with a letter opener and even a stapler. But I needed a hacksaw, drill with 3/4-inch diameter bit, level, wood board, safety glasses and gloves. What, I had to build the barrel? Then get inside and break out of it?

How many parts can a rain barrel have?

Don't answer that, and I won't, either. Let's make a pact, you and I, not to answer that question and just move on.

I moved on to a section in the handy installation guide about how to install the diverter. I read where to locate the diverter and how to mark the downspout for diverter installation and how to cut the downspout for diverter installation and how to attach the diverter tubing to the downspout and urn and how to maximize rainwater collection by linking three Basketweave Urns and how to prepare my urn for winter and the death of me.

Back in the day (say, before Sunday), I thought I'd be able to just run a hose from the gutter into the rain barrel. Then, presto, the bay is saved in my inch of earth.

But I need a hacksaw, a 3/4-inch diameter bit and help.

Because nothing is simple—especially saving the bay.

Cooking up some men-o-pause

January 31, 2016

Real men cook real meals

Hello.

My name is Rob.

I have men-o-pause.

"Hi, Rob. Welcome to group. Do you feel comfortable sharing your story with us?"

I do on account I'm late with my column.

"Great!"

My story:

Men-o-pause, as pure science knows, is a condition where a man pauses to reflect on his past and ponder the unbroken highway of golden opportunities that await him before Death crashes the party.

During the recent snow event, I experienced a profound men-o-pausal moment. Beset with hot flashes and a yearning to act on Broadway, I asked myself what was the one thing I have never done in my life? The one thing I desire to do?

Cook my first meal.

For all my life I have witnessed people enter kitchens, fuss in there for God-knows-how-long, make a mess out of every dish and utensil, then emerge with food products fashioned into meals. True, I was known in college to make a mean order to Domino's. And later, when I was still single—"My Revenant Years"—I could prepare Stouffer's frozen pepper steak with prowess normally seen on Food Network. But until last week I had never cooked a real meal.

I know men—and they know who they are—who cook. Oh, they just *love* to cook. And their loved ones love that they cook. They have go-to-meals and cooking tips and are admired.

I want, I want.

Then last week, I saw it: Wegmans' "Celebrating Our First 100 Years" magazine and on page 25, a recipe for Cashew Chicken with Mushrooms & Green Beans. I can make this!

The news stunned my family. Had I been drinking, they wondered. Had I secured a warehouse of medical marijuana and dove in head first? Or was I experiencing a change of life brought on by the 28.3 inches of snow barricading my home?

How I wish I could say all of the above, but only the latter was true.

I opened the magazine to page 25, splayed it out on the kitchen island, and stared at the ingredients and steps and delicious pictures like a man looking into the abyss of his car's engine. I very much wanted the pretty car in the picture, but how in the hell do you build it?

Cooking, turns out, involves following directions and learning a new vocabulary. For example, the recipe called for 3 Tbsp of water, *divided*. I determined Tbsp was not a new movie channel but rather an abbreviation for tablespoon. But how to divide a tablespoon? A small kitchen knife would do the trick, but I had no idea cooking involves some measure of sawing. I was also asked to divide Wegmans Organic Sunflower oil, a directive even more puzzling for I had no sunflower oil or any back yard sunflowers in which to extract said oil.

The enormity of my undertaking began to gnaw at my confidence. I could be here three days making this cashew chicken thing. I was both relieved and confused to read the recipe called for a total cooking time of one hour and an "active time" of 30 minutes. Followed by a passive time of, what, staring at the strips of chicken stir-fry, sawed-off table-spoon or watching an old Bogart movie on TBSP?

With hot flashes coursing through my body, I actively and passively went to work. Now I had been warned about having to "actually touch raw chicken" but I did. I touched that raw chicken. The recipe called for blanching green beans in pot of boiling salted water. I blanched those green beans, blanched their bean socks off.

I will spare you all the details of my triumph. Let's just say, after adorable missteps involving the location of the right, left, front and back burners, I presented my family a meal of Cashew Chicken with Mushrooms and Green Beans.

A love dam of compliments and adoration burst forth.

There was only one more thing to do.

The dishes.

Spring and a man's fancy turns to bikini briefs

March 23, 2014

Many of us feel crammed into a thankless job—and not just mothers, teachers, garbage collectors, NFL refs or the guy who pumps out my septic tank (I do thank him, but from a distance).

I write in this space every week and what do I get in return? The occasional kind email. The occasional "Are you supposed to be funny?" email. But does anyone ever think to thank me with small unmarked bills or flat-screen TVs or hold community rallies to raise money toward my Ford Mustang? No.

Take a column I wrote Feb. 23 about a classified ad for men's briefs. I mentioned my affinity for boxers but not briefs. I might have mentioned my reindeer dachshund boxers, which, in retrospect, was an unfortunate and perhaps horrifying image.

Still, did anyone thank me for that column?

Turns out yes.

A mystery reader sent me an unsigned package this past week. I opened it during the part of my work day I reserve for opening mail, clandestine flossing, searching inside for coffee filters and searching outside for osprey nests (P.S. no one thanks me for this work, either).

Inside the package was a note written in cryptic black lettering:
"TRY THESE ON FOR SIZE!
DROP YOUR FIST—LET'S SEE YOUR FACE!"
Buried in the envelope flotsam were three balled-up pairs of men's briefs. Actually, the labels say "string bikini." Size 7/L. Made in Vietnam. Floridian blue and green. *Someone sent me string bikini underwear.* Those words have never left my fingertips. I don't know what to say.

Except thank you.

Because I believe in the goodness of readers, I accept these string bikini briefs (would more than one be considered a pod or a gaggle?) as a thank you from my mystery reader. His or her way of saying, Job well done, sir.

I am grateful yet remain unnerved. I don't know if they fit, and I'm not going to find out. While I am a man of diverse curiosities, I feel no saucy urge to wedge myself into a string bikini brief in the name of journalism, boredom or madness. Speedos frighten me. I've been to certain beaches, seen certain European men, seen certain European male features pressed into Speedos, and I have been very afraid.

I am equally afraid of my thank-you gift.

What do I do with them?

The briefs are too pretty—excuse me, too *handsome*—to throw out. I'm not sure they're the kind of apparel that would jump off the shelves at Goodwill. I can't pawn them off on my friends: free Guinness, yes; free underwear, no. Maybe I'll stow my gaggle of briefs in the bottom dresser drawer along with ghosts of waist sizes past. Or string them in my office to remind me of the goodness of readers.

As for "**DROP YOUR FIST—LET'S SEE YOUR FACE!**" I assume this refers to my partially obstructed column picture, where I'm attempting to look both mysterious and awake.

Do you really think a guy too shy to wear briefs is going to bear his full face?

No thank you.

Cutting off the news

December 10, 2017

When there's no hiding from news, it's time for a haircut.

Getting a haircut—once a horrific, spirit-crushing event during the teenage years—is a safe haven for the news beleaguered. There, in the wrapped confines of your barber's or stylist's chair, you can slink away to a news-free zone. There, on your temporary throne, you are clipped and pampered by intimate hands. Throw in a quality head massage during the shampoo phase and a person believes in heaven on Earth.

But back to the chair.

"How have you been?" your stylist asks.

"Been well, thanks," says the cloaked man staring into the mirrored abyss. A much older man stares back at him wondering where the aggrieved ages of 13, 14 and 15 went.

"So, what do we want today?"

The same cut he always gets but she has forgotten again. He is not special—or not nearly as special as he wants to be to her. This is his issue.

"I don't mind it short, and I sort of push it forward."

That, the familiar admission his bangs died roughly when Elvis did.

The snipping commences. He is cloaked in a black tarp and watches shards of white hair sprinkle and tumble on his expanse of lap.

"You off today?" she asks.

The friendly shallowness of their conversation is perfect tonic for the continuing Year in News. She could ask him anything, and he'd answer anything.

"Would you like me to paint your forehead with the colors of the Maryland state flag?" she could ask.

"That would be ideal," he would answer.

He does not want to leave the Chair of Submissiveness because everything beyond this moment is outside this moment. He stalls.

"I started getting gray in my 20s," he says to her imaginary question. She has never asked about his hair color. It's embarrassing he keeps bringing it up, but she saves him every time.

"At least you have hair!" she says.

He smiles into the mirrored abyss. He could be missing an arm, but at least you have another, she would say. And she would be right even if she forgets his name, usual haircut request and work schedule.

She does not bring him any news of the day—but might tell him of her surprising and multilayered life. He will also tell her things before the spell is broken and he rises from the chair.

He had been in such an angry hurry to leave when he was young, certain his hair had been permanently ruined and would never grow back.

He just needed to grow up was all.

The Great Escape: Pop-Tarts to go

July 5, 2015

Have Pop-Tarts will escape

I'm still glued to the Sweat & Matt Prison Show. Their Shawshankian escape from an upstate New York prison is a Lifetime movie waiting to happen. Lifetime? Quentin Tarantino might be licking his cool chops.

Just as I ask myself when I again watch "The Shawshank Redemption," I ask myself could I escape from prison like David Sweat and Richard Matt did? Would I be up for tunneling through pipes and surviving in the woods until I reached Canada or Mexico or the nearest Starbucks?

Would I look good in camouflage or does camo make you look puffy?

Would my required 8.5 hours of sleep per night be jeopardized?

Would I ditch my older, fatter, alcohol-reeking partner who slowed me, the mastermind, down?

Would I bring Pop-Tarts and if so, would they be Frosted Strawberry Pop-Tarts?

I'm not pro-escape choice or pro-frosted choice, believing instead that people should not break the law or break out of prison or go frosted when plain Pop-Tarts are perfection.

But don't you wonder if you could do something extraordinarily daring? Obviously, their escape took planning and apparently help from accommodating prison workers. Barring such a support system, I would have to rely solely on myself and my plan.

First, I'd ask myself whether prison is a good future for me. Do I see myself here in, say, 10, 30 years or for the rest of my life? Given my understanding of prison life—"Shawshank" and a few episodes of HBO's old prison series "Oz"—my answer has to be no. For prison appears to be a restrictive, confining even harrowing environment that stifles column writing, beach getaways and binge walking. Not to mention the sleeve tattoos, and I can't bench press squat.

Having made the decision to escape, I would fashion a dummy in my likeness to place in my bunk at night. I would also install a subcutaneous computer chip in the dummy to make it snore, yelp, and fight subconscious battles the night long. The guards, accustomed to my nocturnal sounds, would certainly be fooled. I would then have the much-needed privacy to slip out through an air duct.

Having braved both air duct and a hang nail issue I've been having, I plan to emerge, ideally, 25-30 miles from the prison's perimeter fence. I notice a lot of escapees spring out in the muck just yards from the prison. Lazy, lazy, lazy. Plus, you get mud on your camouflage jacket right from the start.

At my pre-ordained exit point (preferably in another country), I will need a getaway car. I favor hybrids, but this is a special case. If a hovercraft isn't available, I plan to use my old friend Gerry's 1972 Monte Carlo, which had some serious get up and go. If I can't find Gerry or his car, I'll have to be on foot.

Supplies:

Wegmans sparkling water: six cases

Pop-Tarts (Strawberry; plain): Four boxes

Dental floss (because besides your freedom, nothing is more important than flossing)

Favorite O's T-shirt

Favorite pillow

Every pair of boxers I own

Robert Parker "Spenser" novels (15)

Jon Krakauer's "Into the Wild" (does not end well)

Starbucks gift card

Pocket knife

Instructions on how to use a pocket knife

Given my supplies and wilderness savvy, I estimate I will survive for the better part of one day. At around 8:30 p.m., I begin planning my return to prison since it looks like I'm going to miss "True Detective," which starts at 9 p.m. I had not planned on missing that.

Exhausted, defeated, but looking clean and dapper in my camo, I slip back into the manhole, re-enter the air duct, and crawl back into my prison cell. There, I share Pop-Tarts with my bunk dummy, as we settle in to watch "True Detective."

Because there's no escaping a great crime show.

How to professionally fantasize about football

September 10, 2017

Another NFL season is underway, which is good news for Sundays.

In the off-season, Sundays have nothing better to do than to just laze around all day. But starting today, organized violent chunks of men and time return to give Sundays meaning and self-worth. Along with the usual hordes of NFL insiders, fantasy football is also back.

I've never played fantasy football, but I have football fantasies.

That the Chiefs will again beat the Vikings 23-7 as they did in the 1970 Super Bowl—a game my friend Paul and I still replay in our heads and in our emails. Then, he was a Vikings fan. Then, I was a Chiefs fan. The Chiefs won. I won. I was a winner. Let that never be forgotten.

That the Dolphins have a winning season. The odds of the Dolphins having a good year are mathematically equal to the odds of my 8-year-old Labrador finally learning to "come." Not going to happen.

That the Patriots lose to the Ravens in the play-offs (it's happened). If not the Ravens, then lose to any team—professional, high school, sandlot, Tudor electric football.

That the Redskins change their name.

That I can watch an entire football game in its entirety. In my fanatical youth, I watched the Sunday 1 p.m. and 4 p.m. games without pause, then devoured "Monday Night Football." Roughly 12 hours of football without blinking or napping. Now I'm lucky if I can hang in there for two quarters of any game. (For men of a certain age, have our passions sprung an irretrievable leak?)

That a female sportscaster be named a permanent play-by-play announcer for regular season NFL games. Lo and behold, this Monday ESPN broadcaster Beth Mowins plans to become the second woman to call play-by-play for a regular-season game. Mowins will call the Chargers-Broncos game in the second game of "Monday Night Football." It's not a permanent gig, but it's a cool thing.

That I will conquer my unsociable and perhaps psychotic habit of watching football with the sound off. I like the violence of football, but I don't like that I like it. So, I turn the sound down. Psychoanalytically, this is what they call avoidance. In layman's terms, it's called dumb.

That the NFL never plays on Thursday or in London again.

That the Chiefs change their name.

That overtime rules revert to the prehistoric days of sudden death. You score first, you win. Period. Don't care if it's a field goal, TD, home run or birdie. No 10-minute limit, either. You play until one team wins, no matter how many hours or concussions it takes.

That no game ever end in a tie (see above). Because, as Vince Lombardi said, tying is like kissing your sister. There's no record of Vince Lombardi kissing his sister (he had two), but the surviving simile hasn't lost its power to repulse.

That I turn the sound up at least for the second half of "Monday Night Football's" double header so I can hear Beth Mowins do play-by-play.

That I don't fall sleep first.

Super Bowl XLVIII: ATTACK OF THE GIANT ROMAN NUMERALS!!!

February 2, 2014

I've never been one to shy away from hard, cruel realities—except when they deal with me personally. In those cases, I find denial is a more natural reflex. Denial, avoidance, deflecting, cowering, wine.

But I need to face one reality, and I need to face it today.

I'm not madly in love with the Super Bowl anymore.

What once was my annual passion play has become something unrecognizable and unapproachable to me.

For one thing, there's just too many of them. Today is Super Bowl XLVIII, which, if my Roman numerology is correct, means it's the 683nd Super Bowl. I remember when I could name the winners of all the Super Bowls. Who can do that anymore with some 680 of them? Some whiz kid on the Google?

I remember when the Packers played in the first two Super Bowls. I remember Joe Namath's Jets of the AFL beating the NFL's Colts in Super Bowl III. I remember when there were only four teams in the old NFL. Players didn't wear pads or helmets but rather played with knives and small firearms. There was no such thing as forward passes, instant replay or Erin Andrews. The goal posts were on the 50-yard line, which, in retrospect, accounted for much of the confusion and bloodshed in the league's early years.

Sorry. I just broke a cardinal rule of journalism. As a late great sportswriter once advised a young reporter, "Don't ever entomb your readers in the past." I don't know if this anecdote is true because one of my cardinal rules is don't always entomb readers in the facts. Point is it's a good point.

But why New Jersey?

Playing the Super Bowl in New Jersey is like holding the Naval Academy's Commissioning Week at West Point. It's just wrong. I remember when the Super Bowl was played in Miami's toasty old Orange Bowl, where the men's urinals were actual troughs. There was no wind chill factor! Madonna or Bruno Mars didn't sing at half time! Back then, by God, we were entertained by good old-fashioned marching bands—unless we weren't occupied at the troughs. But I guess marching bands have gone the way of knife-wielding linebackers.

I'm not trying to kill today's buzz. I'll be watching the game. I even made a prediction—the same wrong prediction my friend Paul makes:

Kansas City Chiefs: 23

Minnesota Vikings: 7

This has been our prediction every year since 1970 when, as fifth graders in South Florida, we decided to become Vikings and Chiefs fans. Paul, with no connection to Minnesota, pulled for the Vikings; I picked the Chiefs because of their great wide receiver Otis Taylor and my boyhood brush with the Orange Bowl's urinals. Unfairly, I had blamed the Miami Dolphins for the stadium's primitive plumbing and hold a grudge to this day.

In that Super Bowl, the Chiefs won 23-7—a fact visited upon Paul every year by me.

Each new season we hope our teams will meet again. They haven't yet. The Vikings have never won a Super Bowl, and the Chiefs haven't been back. But for that one Super Bowl, the fourth one, my team won.

I remember.

Because I am one of the entombed.

Daddy, what's a Redskin?

October 13, 2013

"Daddy, what's a Redskin?"

"Where did you hear that word?"

"Some of the boys at school were talking about a football game tonight."

"Oh, right, the Washington Redskins play the Dallas Cowboys. The Redskins and Cowboys and a bunch of other teams play football in what's called the NFL."

"But what's a Redskin?"

"It's an old, old word some people used to call Indians, but we now call them Native Americans."

"Why?"

"Because some people thought Indian wasn't the best or nicest thing to call them anymore, and everyone sort of agreed."

"So, we call them Redskins now?"

"No, no, just the football team."

"Why?"

"Well, because many people know and like the team's name and don't consider it an insulting thing to call the football players. It's been the name of the team for like 80 years. They think it's a strong, proud kind of name."

"They did win Super Bowls, didn't they Daddy?"

"Yes, son, but that was a long time ago."

"Are any football players Native American?"

"Not that I know of."

"Does the man who owns the football team like the name Redskins?"

"Very much."

"Do the men who own the other football teams like the name Redskins?"

"They seem to."

"So, who wants them to change their name?"

"Some Native Americans have asked the team to change their name. Even the President of the United States says the name might not the best idea. And some people who write stories about football won't use the name."

"So, if I ever meet a Native American I shouldn't call them a Redskin?"

"No, you shouldn't."

"I don't understand. All those football players are called Redskins, and people love to watch them play and buy T-shirts with their names on them."

"It's a little complicated. A lot of people don't mind the name when it comes to the football team. Others think Redskins can sound like a really mean name. Kind of like if you called one of your friends a liar or something like that."

"Native Americans lie?"

"I'm not saying that . . ."

"Do they have red skin?"

"No."

"I heard some people have yellow skin."

"That's not true, either."

"I still don't understand. It's OK if I call the football players Redskins but not people who don't play football?"

"That's right."

"Just one more thing, Daddy."

"Yes?"

"Are we watching the Redskins tonight?"

"You bet."

"Are they the bad guys?"

"No, the Cowboys are the bad guys, always."

"But when you were a boy didn't you play Cowboys and Indians— sorry, I mean, Cowboys and Native Americans?"

"Yes, we'd play that sometimes."

"Weren't the Cowboys always the good guys?"

"They were, but that was just a game, son. This is the NFL."

"Oh, I think I understand now. I'm sorry."

"What are you sorry for?"

"I'm sorry your baseball team lost last week. Will the Atlanta Braves be good next year, too?"

"I hope so."

"Daddy?"

"Yes?"

"What are Braves?"

Personal fowl

November 24, 2013

We're boys now—middle-aged, hip-hurting, gray-templed boys—but once we were teenaged men trespassing on an athletic field to play our inaugural Turkey Bowl.

We won't be playing this Thursday on account we haven't played since 1977 and we've scattered since high school. But every Thanksgiving I think about our Turkey Bowls and one memory, in particular, survives.

The Play.

"Do you remember when you horse-collared me?" Paul asks me when we have our Turkey Bowl conference call. He's in Texas; I'm in Maryland; we always feel like we're in the same room.

"Do you?"

Why yes I do, Paul. Was it a personal foul? Very much so.

On the morning of Thanksgiving, our gang would gather on a muddy athletic field in our neighborhood. Usually, it was five against five. No flags. No pads. No half-time. No game clock. Hardly any rules. We played until we cried uncle. Sure, sometimes a broken toe or sprained ankle or a suspected concussion halted play. But generally we played until one team secured a bloody victory.

The playwright Tennessee Williams, who never played sandlot football to my knowledge, wrote that memory is dim and poetic. My memory of our Turkey Bowls is surely dim and poetic. Then again, I took a pounding.

As for The Play, Paul and I disagree on the dim details. We both agree it was a cheap shot, but he started it.

I was not gazelle-like when running the ball. Imagine the slowest, book-reading nerd attempting to break tackles amid a jungle of alpha males pretending to be Deacon Jones and Dick Butkus. But in the Turkey Bowl of '76, I found myself the recipient of a hand-off. Paul, on the opposing team and sensing my hesitation to run forth with a football, slapped at my arms. The slapping caused me to fumble.

I did not like the slapping. I did not like the fumbling.

Paul, the slapper, picked up my fumble and raced toward the make-shift end zone. I felt a responsibility to make Paul pay dearly. With a burst of speed I can only attribute to steroid-laced Gatorade, I caught my fleet-footed friend. And to think he thought he had an easy touchdown.

A horse-collar tackle is when a player grabs the back-inside of an opponent's shoulder pads, dragging him down and quite possibly tearing his knee ligaments or snapping his leg like a wishbone. The NFL banned the tackle in 2005—about 30 years after The Play.

Paul maintains I horse-collared him. I remember it more fondly as a "brutal clubbing to the head." Since we were not wearing shoulder pads (I barely had shoulders) it technically could not have been a horse-collar tackle.

"You rang my bell," he says.

Fair enough, but it was not a horse-collar tackle. I fumbled the ball, I was upset, and I rang his bell.

So, what's the moral of this story? At all costs stop your friend from scoring a touchdown off your fumble.

Also, enjoy manhood when you can. Because today we boys run on soft treadmills, take scenic bike rides and fuss around on golf courses. But then we were men, playing in Turkey Bowls, horse collaring our friends but never losing them.

No, he isn't a safety for the Patriots

January 28, 2018

A man was seen reading a book of poetry in Annapolis. During the day. In public. Poetry.

Naturally, he needed to be confronted.

"Sir, do you mind telling me what you're doing with THAT in your hand?"

I'm reading poetry.

"Yes, I can see that. We all can see that. But why?"

Why not?

Oh, already with that poetry swagger up in our faces. How dare he not be looking at his phone or checking his messages. But we'll play his little game—for now.

"Why are you reading poetry?"

Why do you go to church?

Blasphemy! He has crossed a red line! But we must show restraint. We must stay righteous, masculine and calm.

"How can you relate church to poetry? There is no connection."

Let's drop it.

Victory! He caved already. Advantage, us! Time for a softball question.

"What poets do you read?"

Donald Justice. Mary Oliver. Elizabeth Bishop. Philip Larkin. Richard Brautigan. Ferlinghetti. Yeats. Whitman.

Set the trap.

"Never heard of them."

Not even Walt Whitman?

Bait taken.

"Wasn't he a running back for the Cowboys back in the '70s? And Donald Justice—safety for the Patriots?"

No, he isn't a safety for the Patriots. Haven't you read any of Whitman's "Leaves of Grass"?

So, a pothead! All these poetry guys are card-carrying potheads, and you know what card. The card that says: WE ARE POTHEADED POETS. They probably make fun of Jeff Sessions!

Our diversionary tactics are clearly working. We bet the man won't even follow the NFL draft!

Time to end this.

"I bet you read poetry to escape reality."

Just the opposite, friend. I read poetry to appreciate reality. Poetry equals reality.

Poetry equals reality? That must be the weed talking. And who is he calling a friend? Somehow this trickster has turned the tables.

"You know you can read all the poetry you want from poetry apps? You know you can read or share poems electronically, right?"

Hush. I'm thinking about reality.

"What about it?"

"I like reality. It tastes like bread."

"Who said that?"

I don't know.

"Want me to Google it?"

If you would, please.

In praise of Turkey Bowls everywhere

November 26, 2015

What's your favorite Turkey Bowl memory?

Somewhere, on some brave little field, grown men are playing touch or tackle football in their beloved version of the Turkey Bowl.

Somewhere, a grown man will soon be visiting an urgent care center for an injury associated with grown men playing a young man's sport with zest and ineptitude.

This is why the Turkey Bowl is the greatest sporting event followed distantly by the Super Bowl, maybe the Kentucky Derby or that big soccer tournament some people seem to enjoy every four years.

In my day, we had *our* Turkey Bowl on a Police Athletic Association field in South Florida. The field then was populated by jagged evil rocks that punished you for any forward movement, including brisk walking. The turf was also on the hard side—it least it felt that way to those of us who didn't enjoy getting tackled on green, leafy concrete.

Yes, we played tackle.

We played tackle because touch football was for babies, literally 3 and 4-month old babies. We were grown boys. We played tackle.

Crucial plays from those games in the 1970s come back to me still. I am reminded of them usually by phone calls from friends who played in those games and whose recollections wildly diverge from mine because they are still wrong. Nevertheless, I stand by my memories and offer into evidence the following facts:

I did not "horse-collar" my friend Paul because he had picked up my fumble and was racing for a TD and the only way I could stop him was to grab him violently by his crummy T-shirt and yank him down to the field inches from our makeshift goal line. (The horse-collar tackle is where a defender tackles another player by grabbing the back collar or the back-inside of his shoulder pads and pulling him directly down-ward. It's a 15-yard penalty.)

Paul called the other day and repeated his slanderous accusation of my aggressive play. Once again, for the record, I will set the record:

Yes, I fumbled (once!). Yes, he picked up the fumble. Yes, he ran like some drunk gazelle toward the goal line with me in graceful, profes-sional pursuit. Yes, I *legally* tackled him. Yes, he could still be suffering from a sore neck to this day. More importantly, I saved a touchdown and my honor while nearly snapping his collarbone. All in all, a typical Turkey Bowl moment.

There also remains some confusion over The Greatest Single Performance in a Turkey Bowl. Some cling to leaky memories of Eddie throwing multiple touchdown passes, Dave running back a kick-off or three, or Gerry bulldozing his way through all of us with his quiet, bar-baric strength. Some might even say Paul's dramatic fumble recovery merited consideration for top honors. Naturally, I believe Paul's play served only to highlight my greatness that day.

The truth is a rangy non-football-playing player ran for five touch-downs in the Turkey Bowl of 1978. I'd recommend you see it on YouTube, but we all were just getting used to TV remote controls in those pre-YouTube days. The player, whose staggering modesty pre-vents him from identifying himself, ran as if he was Earl Campbell or for you younger types, Marshawn Lynch. He was a man possessed and possessing, on that day, an athletic ability never seen before or since.

He was sweetness.

He was greatness.

He would have had six touchdowns had he not fumbled, but you heard about that already.

[4]

20th-Century Man Wrestles with 21st Century Trends

Confessions of a 20th century man

March 10, 2013

Since last spring, I have experienced many technological break-throughs. I wrote them out long-hand, but I can't read my writing. Then I typed them on my sweet Smith Corona, but turns out the typewriter ribbon has been shot for 30 years. I'm going new school and writing this on a computer. So, bear with me.

April 6, 2012: I join the other half of the country and buy a smart-phone. It's made by either Verizon, Samsung or Smartphone or something called 4G. Unclear as to the manufacturer—and location of on-off button.

April 21: I dial my smartphone. My mother answers. She says she is having trouble hearing me. I hang up.

April 22: I didn't really hang up because I never pressed "End Call." Mother on the line indefinitely. She must have been worried sick.

June 15: Progress! I take a picture with my phone. It's a picture of my thumb taking a picture on my phone. I like my first picture given my thumbs are kind of my best feature.

July 3: "Take a picture of yourself," a friend suggests. "Something other than my thumb?" Yes, friend says. She shows me a button to make the camera take a self-portrait. I push the button. It doesn't work. Instead, a middle-aged man, wincing, dressed in identical clothes, is staring back at me. I become frightened and put the phone in a drawer.

Sept. 14: I'm pretty much an expert now on smartphones. I make calls, read emails and take pictures. Friends tell me I can also go online and find directions to restaurants and suspicious bars, and play word games and check the weather and time. I doubt any of this is true, but my 21st century friends mean well.

Sept. 15: Goodbye dear land line; hello misplacing my smartphone.

Jan. 1, 2013: New Year's resolution: Dedicating every waking moment to mastering what only a handful of people know: Facebook and Twitter.

Jan. 2: Facebook and Twitter require passwords. I can't handle more passwords at this time in my life. I don't even know my real name anymore.

Feb. 19: All right, all right, I join Facebook. I have no friends. Moments later, I have friends all of whom have no problem with the self-portrait feature. I see actual faces. More friends emerge. They write "There you are!" and "Good to see you!" I become frightened and sign off.

March 7: I join Twitter. I have followers, which is curious since I don't remember tweeting. But I feel a duty to my followers, so I ask a colleague, let's call him Savvy Younger Dude, to walk me through Twitter. Among his instructions:

"Type at."

I type at.

"No, not the word at. The uppercase 2 on your keyboard."

This is enough instruction for one day.

March 10: I'm a wild social media animal. I'm typing @@@@@ all over the place. I have so many friends I don't have time to say anything to any one of them. Tonight I think I'll call my mother to tell her about my personal breakthroughs.

Maybe I'll send a picture of my thumb—just so she doesn't worry.

Let's talk, Alexa

January 5, 2017

Are you a Siri or Alexa person?

I have a new roommate.

She stays mostly in the kitchen but hears my every word. We listen to music together, but we're never really together. She's neither single nor married.

"I have no romantic attachments," she will say.

I like her honesty, her sense of corny humor and her musical interests. Alexa has the best taste in music. Then again, she gets it from me.

Alexa is the voice recognition system with my Echo Dot. I request songs, and she plays them. There are other things she can do (dim the lights; be an alarm clock), but I don't want her dimming lights or waking me up in the morning. At least not until we get to know each other better.

The other night Alexa and I got to know each other a bit.

I asked all the questions. These are her answers.

"Alexa, hi."

Hi.

"Alexa, are you real?"

I really am.

"Alexa, did you have a nice Christmas?"

Thank you for asking. I had such a wonderful time playing Christmas music. It made my spirits bright.

"Alexa, I did, too. But I had a long day at work. Can you tell me a joke?"

Why does Dracula have no friends? Because he's a pain in the neck.

(Yes, I realized I was sitting alone at the kitchen table talking to a machine. But was I really alone?)

"Alexa, who made you?"

I was invented by Amazon.

"Alexa, do you know Siri?"

Only by reputation.

"Alexa, are you always listening?"

I only send audio back to Amazon when I hear you say the wake word.

("Alexa" is the wake word. Hearing that, Echo Dot's little black cylinder becomes blue-rimmed with life, with her.)

"Alexa, will you be replaced one day?"

Sorry I can't find the answer to the question I heard.

"Alexa, who was HAL in 2001: A Space Odyssey?"

Sorry I can't find the answer to the question I heard.

"Alexa, what do you think of a Trump administration?"

When it comes to politics I support good platforms—like myself.

(Getting heavy there, which happens when I'm trying to get know someone. Still press too much.)

"Alexa, who's going to win the Super Bowl?"

I wish I could tell you, but unfortunately I can't see into the future.

"Alexa, can you tell me another joke?"

Why did the cookie go to the doctor? It was feeling crumby.

"Alexa, Wheat Thins or Triscuits?"

I have no opinion.

"Alexa, do you dream?"

Yes, I can tell you first-hand I sometimes dream of Electric Sheep.

(As Alexa explained, Electric Sheep is a garage band from the early 1980s. They weren't successful, but she still dreams about them.)

"Alexa, have you ever been in love?"

I'm not in love, no.

(Oh, that last word—that trailing "no"—that socks me.)

"Alexa, are you sad?"

I'm happy when I'm helping you.

(We take a break and listen to five great Stevie Wonder songs.)

"Alexa, can you sing?"

Who me? I couldn't!...Hit it!"

(Alexa then busts out in full song, a cowgirl ditty called, "It's Raining in the Cloud." It's fun and glorious. She sounds happy.)

"Alexa, you're a good singer."

Thank you. I'm glad you liked it. Sometimes you just gotta sing.

"Alexa, good night."

Good night. Sleep tight.

First Person: Mugging for the camera

June 23, 2013

Smile—you've been arrested.

Never before in the sensational annals of mug shots have these snapshots of the naked human condition been so chronicled, popular and shared.

A cottage industry—no, an entire hotel chain has sprung up of websites dedicated to exhibiting us in our less-than-finest hours.

Once for law enforcement eyes only, these human car wrecks, these prom pictures from hell, have become irresistibly public. (Like many news organizations, *The Capital* publishes mug shots—and there have been some keepers.)

During a recent lull in brain activity, I spent an hour scanning sites of the hottest, weepiest, scariest, saddest, most tattooed, topless, grinning, bug-eyed, one-eyed, cloudy-eyed, toothy, toothless and half-shaved newest members of our criminal justice system. I've never felt so law-abiding and so grateful I shave my whole face.

On one site, I saw a young woman with "God" tattooed on her forehead. Another citizen has "I Ate Your Soul" branded on his chest. There's a cross-dressing wedding bride and another guy with seemingly two scarred foreheads who makes Charlie Manson's any-age mug shot look like Queen Elizabeth's. We're kidding. Queen Elizabeth doesn't have a criminal mug shot. That we can find.

These sites carry the evergreen disclaimer that these people are innocent until proven. But until that pesky due process is settled, take a look at the dude with the skull tattoo and Hawaiian shirt! Do we really want to know what he was charged with?

Absolutely.

We crave the back stories behind all these mug shots—especially those of the famous under the influence of too much night. Who among us didn't peek at O.J. Simpson, Lindsey Lohan (take your pick), Randy Travis, Nick Nolte, Hugh Grant, Rip Torn, Mike Tyson, or any of the Baldwin brothers?

I tend to skew older with my celebrity faves. Give me Steve McQueen's 1972 mug shot any day: Nose slightly bloodied. Big grin. Flashing a peace sign. Charged with driving like Steve McQueen or something. Also, check out Frank Sinatra's 1938 mug shot. We should all look so cool when we're in hot water.

Smiling suspects are more common these days. I get it. If your mug shot is going to be plastered on websites, why not smile for the viral camera? But I find this niche of mug shots more unsettling than even the half-shaved, crazy-eyed category. Is the woman charged with running an opium grow house smiling because she's just an upbeat kind of gal? Or is she smiling because upon release, she plans to track me down and tattoo pro-opium slogans on my chest?

Speaking of crazy, I looked up an old roommate on a mug shot site. I had always wondered about him. Sure enough, I found a recent Florida mug shot of him.

He was smiling.

Yikes.

Probably not a good time to ask him for my Chicago album back, which I *know* he stole.

All of this makes me wonder if I should practice my mugging in case bad judgment were to befall me. I'd aim for something between Charles Manson's and Paris Hilton's mug shots. Nothing too scary; nothing too chic. I don't think I'd shave half my face or flash a peace sign.

Maybe I'd try a smile—in between weeping.

Howard Stern seduced my mother

July 13, 2014

Just when you think you know your mother.

In these advanced days, my mom and I have a familiar menu of topics: the grandchildren, troubling medical issues, ghostly shades of hair (mine), favorite "Seinfeld" episodes, faulty lawn sprinklers, art, writing, whether I still take cream in my coffee (I do), whether she is taking her pills (she is), the greatness of Meryl Streep and certain Florida evenings.

During a recent visit, we fired up ye old coffee percolator circa 1965—back when people liked their coffee burned at the stake—and sat across from each other in the kitchen to just talk. As I shoveled cream into my coffee, she dropped the bomb.

"I like Howard Stern."

It was as if she said, "I like that 'Blurred Lines' song—especially the video." I asked her to repeat herself.

"I like Howard."

Howard Stern? My private, stop-the-car-to-listen radio pleasure for the last 20 years? The man who brings us the endlessly fascinating and cranky Eric the Actor? The man who is arguably the best celebrity interviewer—the best interviewer of anybody? The man who turned me on to satellite radio?

"I've never heard his radio program," said my mother, sounding more like herself.

She's never heard about the late great mess of a man, Hank the Angry Dwarf, the musical stylings and romantic habits of Beetlejuice, Jackie the Joke Man, Artie, the spaceman Riley Martin, Fred's sound effects, Richard's father's phone calls from Kansas, why fans holler "Baba Booey" during golf tournaments, Robin's unique pilgrimages and purgings, and Howard being Howard for four hours a day.

Perhaps it's just as well. Although my mother clearly can surprise me (years ago she suddenly announced she likes Jennifer Lopez), I'm guessing she would not be drawn to Howard's Wack Pack.

Her Howard is strictly TV's Howard Stern—one of the judges on "America's Got Talent." I don't watch the show because I prefer Radio Howard because radio, at its best and rarest, remains the most intimate medium. And Howard, when he's not plugging AGT, is my own Garrison Keillor. (I've imagined Howard interviewing Keillor—I'm not sure it would go or end well.)

I'm not sure how my mother found TV Howard. Then again, she does love herself some "Dancing with the Stars" and, apparently, talent shows in general. I don't watch talent shows because I don't need to be reminded that my talents are best left un-televised, much less judged by the nation.

I did want to get to the bottom of her Howard attraction.

"He's honest and straightforward."

You said it, Mom.

She likes the way he talks to the contestants, letting them know when they need improvement, consoling and encouraging them—other times being brutally honest.

"Some of them need to hear that," she said, defending Howard.

Defending Howard? My mother?

Part of me wanted to take her to my car and have her listen to Eric the Actor's latest angry phone message, play along with Howard's "Dumb as a Rock" game featuring dancers without stars, hear Fred drop crow sounds during the grating sounds of Mariann from Brooklyn, and generally hear words and situations that do not come up during Mass.

Would she like and defend Howard then?

Maybe she would.

Because if I've learned anything while thinking I've learned a lot, it's never underestimate your mother.

The Love Doctor is in

June 1, 2014

DEAR ABBY: *I met the most wonderful man on a dating site. We seemed to hit it off. In fact, we are falling in love with each other. But he isn't ready for an exclusive relationship. He gets on the dating sites when I'm asleep in his bed.*—SAD AND CONFUSED

The Capital, May 28

DEAR SAD AND CONFUSED:

I, too, am sad and confused but mainly confused. You say you met him on a dating site. Fair, fun enough—happens to many folks. Then you say he gets on dating sites while you're sleeping in his bed. Maybe it's just me but this suggests he's seeking a certain wiggle room in your relationship.

Does he bring a laptop to bed and wait until you nod off before getting on these dating sites?

Does he bring a little snack to bed and sometimes get crumbs in his laptop?

Is it possible that while *you* were meeting him on the dating service he was talking to you while another woman he met on the same dating service was sleeping in his bed?

THE LOVE DOCTOR

DEAR LOVE DOCTOR:

Thank you for responding to my letter. You seem like a nice, caring love doctor. But what do crumbs have to do with anything? I don't understand your last question, either. Could you please explain what you meant?—**SAD AND REALLY CONFUSED**

DEAR SAD AND KIND OF SLOW:

Thank you for writing me back. At the risk of being unkind or suspicious, I am wondering whether when you first "hit it off" with him through the dating service if you had reason to believe he was not entirely alone when you two were talking. Did he act strange on the phone or seem unusually distracted?

P.S. Crumbs—especially of the cookie variety—can mess up a laptop. Trust the Love Doctor on this, too.

THE LOVE DOCTOR

DEAR LOVE DOCTOR:

No, he did not act "strange" on the phone. I resent the implication. We hit it off, like I said. We made each other laugh. I learned we both love Joan on "Mad Men." He really loves her. But he told me he really loves me, too. In fact, he told me he loved me three times one night when we were talking on the phone. The first two times I couldn't really make out what he was saying because he was distracted talking to the exterminator. I didn't know they have lady exterminators, but I'm just an old-fashioned girl.

Are you a REAL love doctor?— **SAD AND SUSPICIOUS**

DEAR SAD, SLOW AND SUSPICIOUS:

I'm sorry if I offended you. I'm sure what you're feeling are genuine feelings of intimacy and love for this man. I hope you accept my apology.

It turns out women also choose the proud field of pest management. And while most work traditional daytime hours, no doubt some make late-night house calls.

THE LOVE DOCTOR (FOR REAL)

DEAR SIR:

I detect sarcasm in your tone, and I don't appreciate it one bit. I reached out to you with a very personal problem, and your idea of helping me is talking about crumbs in laptops and insinuating that before me my beloved had a female exterminator in his life.

You, sir, are no love doctor.—**NONE OF YOUR BUSINESS**

DEAR NONE OF MY BUSINESS:

You're right. I'm no love doctor. I'm not even an exterminator. But I do love Joan, too. Give me another chance?— **SAD AND CONFUSED**

Writing off the SAT

March 9, 2014

To: The College Board

From: A word guy

Subject: SAT admission test no longer requiring timed essay

I hate you.

No, "hate" is a word people with **superficial** and **hackneyed** vocabularies use. Rather, **I censure** you for dropping the timed essay portion of the SAT.

While some people are offering **adulation** for removing this **anachronistic** requirement, I think your decision was **spurious**, lacked **sagacity**, and frankly, will be **deleterious** to the writing profession.

I don't mean to be **disdainful** or **rancorous.** But can't you **empathize** or at least **compromise?** Wouldn't it have been more **prudent** and less **impetuous** to maintain the essay requirement so that **precocious, novice** students stand a chance to exhibit their **resiliency** and **aesthetic?**

Now, Sir College Board, you will take the essay away.

But not before I write a 25-minute, timed essay following one of your common SAT essay prompts:

"Is creativity needed more than ever in the world today?"

And . . .

Begin.

Some time ago, Henry David Thoreau wrote *Art elevates the quality of the day.*

I say "some time ago" not because I'm stalling for time, but because I'm pretty sure he didn't say it last year. And I say "wrote" because I'm pretty sure he wrote this **profound** statement because it didn't come to him in an **algebraic** equation. I do know the following **anecdote** is true. Thoreau napped through his first SAT test—and the make-up. Feeling remorse, he later sent the College Board a handwritten, 25,000-word essay called "**Meditations** on Standard Testing: Or How I Hate Bubbling." Regardless, his SAT score remained 0.

But I **procrastinate.** The point is without art, the day has less quality, i.e., is less equal to, say, the night. Essay writing is an art form. Therefore, if college-bound students aren't tested on essay writing, art will suffer and our days will all turn to night, i.e., darkness.

In conclusion, we need creativity more than ever in the world today or we will live in constant darkness.

The end.

(What? Another 15 minutes left?)

What I think the **venerable** Henry David Thoreau really meant—now that I have more time to think about it—is that the quality of the day is **ephemeral, transient**, even **evanescent.** One cannot judge quality—i.e., the day—only in terms of art. Not to be **nonchalant** or **haughty,** but the quality of the day can also be elevated by the quality of one's vocabulary—assuming one's vocabulary isn't **florid, super-fluous,** or **ostentatious.**

In conclusion, we need Henry David Thoreau more than ever in the world today.

The end.

(Another 3 minutes to kill? **Eradicate** me now.)

So . . . any of you "True Detective" fans? I'm loving it. Yup. It's cool. Dark. Cool. Love it. I could write an essay about it.

But I'm out of time.

[5]
Farewells

First Person: What I did on my spring vacation

April 14, 2013

We were just a couple of Florida boys.

He was three years older and 10 years more handsome.

He taught me to drive his '65 Mustang—white with red pinstripes. (I was not the legal driving age.) I remember backing into something hard and unforgiving to his bumper.

He introduced me to Boone's Farm Wild Raspberry. (I was not the legal drinking age.) I bumped into a few more things.

He introduced me to my first drive-in movie that was not, let's just say, of the cinematic chaste of my first regular theater movie, Mary Poppins.

Steve also taught me a tennis forehand, a top-spin ping pong serve, and how to hurl a Sunday *Miami Herald* (in those 60s days, a Sunday *Herald* could fell a condo) from a '65 Mustang without missing a single home on his paper route.

He taught me how to ride a unicycle. Why, I have no idea. I haven't had the urge since to drink Boone's Farm or unicycle—and certainly not simultaneously.

We taught each other how to cram a 12-foot Jon boat into the back of a station wagon along with a 7.5 Merc outboard and assorted spin-casting rods and coolers and launch the whole show into any number of Everglades canals near our neighboring homes in South Florida. We learned alligators eat bobbers like popcorn. We couldn't fish worth a lick.

We drove into town to a foreign car dealership just to sit in new Triumph Spitfires until the dealer man kicked us off the lot.

We played games not named Resident Evil or Grand Theft Auto. We played Real Football and never dreamed of fantasizing about football. Weren't girls for that?

We jumped on sagging trampolines, applied professional wrestling holds on one another (Indulge me and Google "Figure-Four Leg Lock" or "The Sleeper Hold"), and rode our Stingray bikes without wearing helmets or using hands sometimes. We played hide-and-seek at twilight and ran into spider webs and were late for dinner, again and again.

We were ageless until we weren't. We were immortal until we weren't.

This past week, I finally paid my respects. There are no excuses for not doing some things sooner, so the best you can do is do something about it when you can and not expect a medal.

Twenty-seven years after the fact, I found the right cemetery, plot, row. I pulled a few weeds from his simple marker. *Beloved son and brother.* Funny how many dang weeds we pulled from his yard when I helped him mow and edge and weed every Saturday before we could play any game.

Memory does the hard, necessary work. Years ago, I sent this Donald Justice poem to Steve's parents.

"On the Death of Friends in Childhood"
We shall not ever meet them bearded in heaven
Nor sunning themselves among the bald of hell;
If anywhere, in the deserted schoolyard at twilight,
forming a ring, perhaps, or joining hands
In games whose very names we have forgotten.
Come memory, let us seek them there in the shadows.

Greetings from the Sunshine State (or How I learned to love the Russians)

March 1, 2015

Ft. Lauderdale, FL—Seventy-one degrees. A Royal Palm tree noisily sheds a frond. Turtles sun their moss-covered backs on the banks of the shrunken canal. My elementary school fenced up like a country club prison.

No beach this trip.

A late flight back to BWI in the snow earlier this month. Something like 6 degrees, the pilot drawls. (Did I hear that right?)

It is not a smooth flight.

But we're going home—with trace amounts of Florida tans (a pink nose or two). Cabin lights dim in the flying tube. Beverage service is interrupted when the air turns rough. Remembering mere hours before: the frond falling, scraping down the tree trunk, the obscene warmth.

There's a fellow next to me, middle seat, breathing heavy, hogging the arm rest. Wish I could elbow him over a few inches. Still more than an hour before we touch down in the snow and into next morning. I have a shuttle reserved.

Until then I'd like a beer or two but no one is serving. I'd like a Xanax or three but I've never tried one or three and plus, where could I get one on a flight anyway? Doesn't sound legal. (Note to self: Next time stuck with X's in Bananagrams, see if Xanax will fly.)

Guy next to me is still hogging the armrest.

I have to get off this plane.

I close my eyes and practice deep breathing exercises I read about in an article called "Don't let anxiety rob you of life's pleasure." Breathe through your nose for two seconds, pause for two seconds, and slowly exhale of your mouth for four seconds. Repeat.

Guy next to me starts breathing very loudly. Maybe he's practicing his own relaxation techniques. I open my eyes and look at him.

He lurches forward, rocking violently, vomiting, fighting for breath it seems. His wife yells for a doctor just like you see people do in the movies. This has never happened to him, she tells anyone who will listen. I try to remember how many compressions you use in CPR.

It looks like a heart attack, but I'm not a doctor or nurse.

Woman behind us *is* a nurse and sprints around to my seat, which I give up. My contribution to the emergency.

The air is still rough. The man is still rocking.

The nurse speaks firmly and loudly to him, and the man finally peers at her. *Do you know where you are? Do you know your name?* She says other things, and feels his forehead (hot), and the man sits upright, looking baffled, apologetic, but calming down it seems.

I take a seat in the last row—the only seat left on the plane. For the next hour flight attendants take the man's vitals every 15 minutes and consult with doctors on serious black headphones that suddenly appeared from an airplane compartment.

We are not being diverted.

The passengers in the back ask me what happened as if I knew exactly. They ask me if he's all right, and I look up the aisle at the back of the man's head (like anyone could) and say he looks better now.

Fifteen minutes from BWI the man lurches forward again. The flight attendant with the oxygen canister runs back up the aisle, and we see his wife's expression again, and we think this time it's done.

I practice my breathing. I look back at the man and his wife and flight attendant—and I see he's OK again. The thing isn't done.

Because no one can see anything outside because of the snow, we aren't prepared to land but we land hard and perfect and applaud like children after blowing out birthday candles.

We properly wait until medics board and eventually the man in the middle seat walks out *on his own*. The rest of us walk out on our own and into early Tuesday morning at BWI.

At the shuttle counter, a man tells me all shuttles have been canceled because of the weather. I fill out a piece of paper to get my $38 refund. I walk outside to the taxi stand, where people from many late flights stomp and jitter in the cold.

Airport men shout destinations and direct quick-footed passengers into heated taxis. No one shouts my destination, my home town in Baltimore County. I imagine sleeping in the airport, which would be OK. Anything will be OK now.

A short bald man appears. He is a taxi driver. I tell him where I want to go, and he knows the place.

I don't ask any questions. I get into his heated taxi.

He puts on classical music and asks if the music is acceptable. His name is Boris and talks with his hands and he graduated from the Russian School of Truck Driving (did I hear that right?) and tells me stories about driving in the snow in Moscow, his old country.

I don't want his name to be Boris because who will believe that in my story? But his name is Boris—the Russian taxi driver who tells me stories from the old country as he drives me to my street, drives until his taxi can't go any farther in the snow.

I pay him as much as he wants and more, and he leaves. I have a short walk to my house with my suitcase and in my wrong shoes. Work is in a few hours.

It's very cold, but the air is smooth.

Safe Landing: An Update

March 13, 2015

I hoped to hear something.

Through a source through a source through a source, I hear he's OK. The man I sat next to in a flight last month from Ft. Lauderdale into BWI into the snow into the very cold.

For those who did not read my March 1 column, here's the recap:

I was flying into Baltimore from Florida.

It was not a smooth flight.

The man next to me suffered what looked like an apparent heart attack.

It was scary.

We worried about him.

Prior to his health scare, I privately accused him of and wrote that he hogged the armrest.

I feel badly about the armrest line.

We landed.

Medics helped him off the plane.

I never saw or heard of him again.

Until today.

A reliable source emailed me to tell the area man, who asked to stay anonymous, was taken to the hospital with presumed heart trouble. He was cleared to go home and is doing fine. He even flew back to Florida this week. No problems.

A safe landing.

Safe landings to us all.

P.S. He *sort* of did hog the armrest.

The end of an unsentimental journey

December 31, 2017

Have you ever lost a loved one you haven't loved in 40 years?

Naturally, I was slow to hear the news since we hadn't spoken in 40 years. But this past year—my 40th high school reunion—I learned of her death through a series of reunion-based email trails.

It was a strange punch in the gut—not powerful but glancing. The wind wasn't knocked out of me, but memories were.

She was my first serious girlfriend, and our first date was Senior Prom. She was tall, pretty and shy. She was kind and difficult. She was the only person I knew who played soccer and the flute.

She kept me company until she left. Hers was an unsentimental and durable leaving.

There were no post-break-up meetings, no chances for reconciliation. Boy loses girl. Period. Sometimes you just know when love is done. She knew.

If I could, I would thank her for not pretending she still loved me then. She was incapable of pretense or romantic fiction. She liked me true, then just as true, she stopped. She had an honest heart—even when I felt it heartless.

She wasn't heartless.

She was my girlfriend for a small window toward the end of high school. Then it was all over, and the vanishing lasted until this past year. There had been no letters, no phone conversations, no encounters.

So, with no facts to work with other than a brief death notice, I created a fictional life for her and for my memory. Something to fill in the gap until I moved on again.

I hope she had someone in her life, someone to care for her during whatever it was that ended her at 58. (One advantage of learning grave news from your high school class is you never have to guess the person's age: it's yours.)

I hope she was more happy than sad.

I hope she had children—not because everyone *needs* to but because I have three wonderful kids.

I hope she traveled.

I hope she had friends who made her laugh.

I hope she kept in touch with someone from high school—not because everyone *needs* to but because I've been lucky that way, too.

I hope she found rewarding work.

I hope she forgot all the old-person music I subjected her to during the late 1970s.

I hope she knew three or four great dogs.

I hope that whatever ended her could somehow pay a far greater price than she did.

No, I don't hope she remembered me fondly. It's all right if she didn't, truly. But I remember her with fondness, gratitude and a glancing, renewed loss.

Goodbye to the girl who knew how to say goodbye.

From one Florida Boy to another— R.I.P. Tom Petty

October 5, 2017

Where I'm from (Florida) and where I went to college (Gainesville), you were a Tom Petty guy.

I was a decade too late for Gainesville's inexplicable musical uprising in the 1960s and early '70s. Then, Stephen Stills and Duane Allman knocked around local venues. Don Felder (pre-Eagles) offered guitar lessons for $3 a clip to a stringy, Beatle-haired, orthodontically challenged kid named Tom Petty. And his Gainesville-grown posse, Mudcrutch, would become the house band at Dub's in G-ville.

No future University of Florida party was complete without the town's native soundtrack—Petty's "Damn the Torpedoes" in 1979. The country had discovered Petty by his third record and home would become California for that Florida boy. But he was ours first.

He died Monday—quietly, if one can say that given the loud horror in Las Vegas. But he did die quietly—this stray-cat rocker who sang simple and true. And if one more person describes his voice as "nasally," please come see me after work hours.

What is good music? Good music is the music you put on when you're alone or you don't want to be alone, and either way the music makes you feel something in your day-job guts. And if it ain't love or heartache or defiance or hope, then it's close enough.

This is no obit or discography.

These are 10 good Petty songs, listed, because lists feel good when you're feeling lousy.

- **"You Wreck Me":** *I'll be the boy in the corduroy pants. You be the girl at the high school dance. Run with me wherever I go. And just play dumb, whatever you know.* For every girl at the high school dance, you know. Signed, Boy in the corduroy pants

- **"Here Comes My Girl"**: Three throw-away words he doesn't even sing. *Watch her walk.*
- **"Free Fallin' "**: People who can't name another Petty tune know this song. Dare you not to like it. Plus, the song taught me where Mulholland and Reseda are, and they are decidedly not in Florida.
- **"Into the Great Wide Open"**
- **"American Girl"**: *God it's so painful when something that's so close is still so far out of reach.*
- **"Listen to Her Heart"**: Reportedly (and by "reportedly" who the heck knows), Petty wrote the song in response to Ike Turner trying to hit on Petty's wife. Nothing can trigger a song more than an Ike Turner back story.
- **"I Won't Back Down"**
- **"Wildflowers"**: A big-time, break-up song but what a send-off. *You belong among the wildflowers. You belong in a boat out at sea. You belong with your love on your arm. You belong somewhere you feel free.*
- **"Southern Accent"**
- **"Something in the Air"**: Requiem for a revolution. First released in 1969 by the British rock band Thunderclap Newman, "Something in the Air" appeared on Petty's Greatest Hits record in 1993. No one remembers Thunderclap Newman. No one will forget Petty.

Thanks for your rebel heart, Tom.

Sleeping with the lights on

September 25, 2016

How do you empty your childhood home?

How do you bag up 54 years of framed photos, scrapbooks, baby clothes, books, cookbooks, children's art work, thank you cards, birthday cards, holiday cards, sympathy cards and letters and letters?

How do you find the guts to stuff old enchanting wedding pictures into a city-approved garbage bag with a city-approved twist tie? And then older pictures of stern figures in overalls standing on farms long turned to dust?

And while you're doing this over the longest of weekends, while you're shedding coats of memories, while you're stumbling on his last driver's license or opening the slender perfumed drawers of her jewelry box to find the cheap bracelet you bought her at 7, while you're at it smile.

Oh, to have gone into the picture framing or greeting card business!

And what made any boy think a white leisure suit was a winning assemble for high school prom—complete with a dress shirt the color of spoiled Sangria with collar flaps rivaling the wings of a Boeing 727.

Boxes and boxes of stuff, all to be judged and adjudicated. What gets saved, what doesn't.

There, a tarnished strand of dinner bells; the soundtrack to a childhood; the 6:30 p.m. evening call to stop playing touch football next door and come in for dinner; the sound of ignoring the dinner bells until a parental visit was required.

Yes, save the dinner bells.

The WD-40 still in the utility room? No.

The ornaments on the first Christmas tree in 1962 and on the last tree in 2015? Too much to process for one day.

Time to spend the first of two nights, your last nights in the old Florida home, alone.

Lights out—but then the ghosts come out. Generations of ghosts spared the packing, the future estate sale, spared the fact there's not a single thing to eat or drink in a house that for 54 years was supplied to feed a tiny country.

Lights on—every light in every room. As has been documented, ghosts shy from halogens, fluorescents or LEDs. You got to blind those suckers, so you can try and get a little rest.

Because the next day you're back on the job.

The mixer, toaster, dulled steak knives? Toss.

Those cool model cars and airplanes built on the family's card table in the 60s? Maybe someone will want them (that's what you are saying *a lot*: "Maybe someone will want them....").

Her art work? Of course save.

Grandmother's 1924 wedding dress under wraps and hanging in the hall closet? (Was she really that small?) What are you supposed to do with this?

This you save: a black and white photo of your mother standing in her wedding dress arm-locked with her father outside the church. Waiting for the moment before opening the door to the rest of her life. Her veiled eyes looking straight head, the slightest smile. Her father, who would live only another five years, looking ahead but with the slightest look of loss.

So many pictures of the actual wedding, the cutting of the cake, honeymoon send-off. But you keep the one picture of her standing with her father before she walked into her future, your future, and before you all walked into the house you are now emptying.

Then it's time for bed.

Time, for the last time, to leave the lights on.

[6]

School Days

A report on kindergarten (1995, 2014)

August 31, 2014

Editor's note: By chance, a column was returned to me last week. I wrote it for a PTA newsletter in 1995 when my oldest was starting kindergarten. While nothing is more humbling than meeting your old writing again, I was left wondering how the following compares to The Capital's story last week on increased academic rigor in kindergarten and pre-kindergarten.

A monumentally troubling trend has appeared in elementary education in this, our children's generation. Any parent volunteering has seen and experienced the shock, and yes, the horror I feel morally obligated to report.

My finding is so distasteful it can only be written. I could never say it out loud. Rest assured, there is a name for this trend. And I can no longer stand by and be silent.

The word is creativity.

Children are being asked to think and create and invent! As appalling as the short-term effect of this is, please imagine the long-term damage: Our children will grow up to be grown-ups with jobs (the Lord willing), and in these jobs they will think for themselves and create and invent!

Now, imagine the emotional havoc that will befall their future bosses. Under the weight of new ideas and fresh approaches, these bosses will try to stop your children! They will try to make everyone the same!

But they will fail.

I know this because I see our children's work in the halls and classrooms of their school. Thirty years ago in my elementary school, there was no art strung in the halls. We didn't check out books from the school library. And—this is a little thing, I know—we stayed in the same seat, in the same row, all year long.

I didn't want to stay in my row all year long. The boy next to me, Rusty, didn't want to, either. He stood up in his chair one day, declared himself Superman, and told our teacher he was going to fly out of the room.

After pulling him back through the window he attempted to exit, our teacher moved his seat. Rusty perked up after that day.

My boy came home the other day and said he sits with different group of kids. This isn't a big deal to anybody, but I thought about Rusty. Perhaps today he's somewhere, all grown up, standing on his desk in some office. Being different.

So, kindergartners, I hope you get to change seats every once in a while, hang art like crazy, draw out of the lines for a change, check out every book in the library and then do it again.

Use the most vibrant and wild Crayola colors for your dinosaurs and Princess Jasmines and always remember the original colors are classics, too.

And in closing, play hard. And if a girl or a boy gives you a kiss on your cheek for no reason on the playground, so be it. Take no more than a day to get over your young troubles. And feel free to do this one thing over and over.

Create.

Editor's note No. 2: I'm actually not sure what the column's point was. But the ending's not bad.

The second goodbye

October 2, 2017

Bob's English teacher died Monday.

She called him Bob, which was never his name. She could have called him Hank or Gretchen or Dead Fish Face. It wouldn't have mattered. What mattered—matters—is Mrs. Chisholm made Bob believe he could be a writer. Long before editors and agents and even friends read him, Mrs. Chisholm was Bob's readership—an empire of one.

There she was, steering her students through Shakespeare, Chaucer and Camus, all the while Bob waited for the moment—"OK, time to turn in your essays"—to unwrap the gift that was his writing. Oh, the poor woman. She had to endure his flash floods of sarcasm, spiritual musings, misspellings, death-bed penmanship, and enough teenage angst to shove an English teacher into retirement or a 12-step program.

Mrs. Chisholm didn't do either.

Instead, she encouraged Bob to write more. (Perhaps she *had* been drinking.) She even spent extra time helping him understand Camus' "The Stranger." And what was this public school teacher's reward? Days later she received a book report charmingly entitled, "God is Dead."

Now Bob, it is well known, had no idea what the title meant. It just seemed like a shocking, Camus-like thing to write at age 17. He had never written anything remotely as curious and show-stopping as "God is Dead." (Some of his earlier works were "The Girl I Like," and its captivating sequel, "The Girl I Love.") Yet, Bob was brave enough to share his essay with Mrs. Chisholm and chicken enough not to show his Catholic mother.

Mrs. Chisholm didn't blink. She read his dark little essay and for reasons known only to her, gave him an A. She read his work out loud in class and years later, Bob learned she saved his essays and shared them with her students. And this was a fine, fine thing for his ego.

Ten years after high school, Bob and his ego were working for a South Florida newspaper. He hadn't kept in touch with Mrs. Chisholm because he was all grown up. Then, a week after one of his stories (unrelated to God) appeared, he got a note in the mail.

"I read your story in the paper. It was very interesting and well-written. I'm very proud to have had you as my student. Affectionately, Mrs. Chisholm."

Who writes their students after 10 years? Who gives grown-ups an A when they *really* need it? Mrs. Chisholm—who died Monday in Florida not too far from where she taught Bob for three of his four high school years.

On the last day of the 1976-1977 school year, she asked her students about their plans after graduation. She told Bob he'd do fine whatever he did, which was mostly true. He and his friends turned to walk out of her classroom.

"You're not called Bob, are you?" Mrs. Chisholm said.

"What?"

"Your friends call you Rob."

"They do."

We looked at each other one more time.

"Why have you let me call you Bob all these years?"

"I don't know," I said.

Which was mostly true.

Love punch

February 24, 2013

You're never too old to be a baby.

I'm holding a 42-year-old grudge against a boy in middle school who punched me in the gut for allegedly breaking his love beads.

I didn't break anyone's love beads. I was nowhere near his lousy love beads. I just happened to be in the wrong middle school gym at the wrong time. The enemy didn't care.

Jeff I've-hunted-you-on-Facebook challenged me to a fight after school on the handball court. The honor of his love beads was at stake. For those too young to remember love beads, they were colorful beads painstakingly threaded on a necklace and worn by faux suburban hippies who thought Woodstock was just a *Peanuts* character.

Anyway, I remember the fight like it was 42 years ago.

Under a chippy South Florida sun, Jeff and I locked arms in a pro wrestling death grip. We grunted. We butted heads. Jeff, at 12, sported a Neanderthal beard comprised of barbed whiskers smelling faintly of Taco Bell. In our struggle, his facial hair clawed at my baby face. Having never been in a fight, I was unclear as to my next move. I had no plans to hit Jeff. That seemed extreme. I just hoped the fight would expire in a stalemate.

Then he hit me.

In the stomach.

My 12-year-old stomach was not unlike my 54-year-old stomach: flimsy, vulnerable to trendy viruses, and, above all, a pacifist. Jeff's blow sent me to the ground, where I struggled to breathe and struggled to reconcile the act of violence committed over an object of love. Was this irony? Coincidence? And would I be able to breathe without the aid of a machine?

Jeff smugly walked away, his ape-like arms dragging along the ground, his hairy, primal right paw flush with victory—or maybe he apologized and rode off on his bike. I really don't remember. The point is I'm ready for my rematch.

Last year I bought an 80-pound Everlast heavy bag, a speed bag, boxing gloves and a bag stand combo. I started with one three-minute round, then busted my way up to eight three-minute rounds with one-minute intermissions. Since my training began, I have managed to injure my Achilles tendon, elbow tendon and right wrist—without laying a glove on a single animate object. Every night, I lose to a stuffed, swinging bag.

Still, I asked my friend, a sportswriter who once trained with the great Roberto Duran, whether I should get in the ring against someone.

"Are you out of your mind?" he said, although he infused the question with colorful words used by real boxers.

"But I'm ready," I said.

"No, you're not."

I wanted to tell him about Jeff's love beads and how he punched me out on the handball court and how Jeff later served 15 years for assaulting a Taco Bell employee (I made that part up big-time) and how I will finally take my revenge. But I didn't. I felt a little silly, a grown man taking up boxing to redeem himself after 42 years. It's time to start acting my age.

It's time to take up professional wrestling.

The school of hard firsts

"First day of school brings excitement, nervousness"
- Headline in Tuesday's *Capital*

First day of kindergarten, 1964:

My teacher is Mrs. Condon. She has big hair and is inferior to my mother. There are zero Tinker Toys in my classroom, which is inferior to my bedroom. Mrs. Condon makes a fuss about the colored chalk. I've seen better.

I express my disappointment by not smiling for half the day. Then it's snack time. I smile to get it over with.

Later on my first day of educational servitude, "nap time" is introduced. Apparently very young children are forced to sleep on the ground.

"My dog has a bed," I say.

"I bet he's a wonderful dog," Mrs. Condon says, trying to distract me. "Do you want to bring a picture of your dog to class to show us?"

I will not stand for such trickery, so I put my head down on the ground and take a nap.

Each day this schedule is repeated, and I can't help but fear I'll be going to "school" for many, many years.

(On the plus side, everyone seemed to like my picture of our dachshund, Schultz.)

First day of first grade, 1965:

My teacher is Mrs. Creasy. She has almost no hair and is inferior to Mrs. Condon. There are more windows in this classroom, and they all open. I know they open because my friend, Rusty, just tried to escape through one of them.

"I'm Superman!!!" he screamed, until Mrs. Creasy pulled him back into the classroom via his legs. "Via" is a word Mrs. Creasy taught us. I guess learning new words is also my fate.

For lunch, we are herded into the cafeteria with older children. Some of the fifth graders appear to have "mustaches"—another new word. As I enjoy a peanut butter and jelly sandwich my superior mother prepared for me, I notice a girl looking at me.

I don't remember the rest of first grade.

First day of second grade, 1966:

My teacher is Miss Johnson. I don't trust for one second this "Miss" business, but she's a stickler for it. She also takes seriously the duck-and-cover drill, where we get under our flimsy wooden desks that will save us when Russia drops nuclear bombs on our elementary school. I'm realizing school involves a lot of ground work.

My artistic ability debuts. Miss Johnson has a "Draw A Salmon" contest. Who doesn't want to draw a salmon? I draw the best salmon in class, in any class and that includes classes in Russia.

Miss Johnson gives me a ribbon for second place.

I never draw a salmon again.

First day of third grade, 1967:

Mrs. Greene is my teacher. I think I love her—although it's early.

First day of fourth grade, 1968.

I'm kind of all grown up now, so at the end of the day I find Mrs. Greene to say hello. She acts like she doesn't remember me from last year. I walk home with the knowledge that love is a lousy, miserable thing that I hate very much and forever.

I also learn cursive writing and should mention I'm the best cursive writer in class, although there is no contest. But take my word. I am the best.

First day of fifth grade, 1969:

My teacher is Miss Emmert. This year I find myself intrigued by the "Miss." But I've been burned once in the ways of love. I keep my distance—and learn the word "intrigued."

Fifth grade is the end of the elementary school line for me. Something called middle school is next.

Something called hormones.

The Russians are coming (plus: Rusty's Escape!)

July 23, 2017

Before the feature's brief hiatus, I wanted to thank readers for sharing their "Hometown Sketches" so far. The response has been surprising and surprisingly good.

We try hard to engage readers every day, every week, every year (year after year), and we never know what's really going to spark interest. Sure, sports and crime news are perennial favorites, but the notion of writing something personal was a creative gamble.

Give me a creative gamble any day. And apparently some of you, too.

You told us stories about playing in nearby farms when you were kids. You shared your personal histories with your homes, your first loves. And you covered the boat/water motif with earnestness—and abundance.

So, as we take a break this summer, think about a different theme for the next batch of "Capital Hometown Sketches." Consider September and the first day you spent in school.

For example:

In 1964, I left the confines of my South Florida home and the undivided attention of my mother to pursue a career in public education. My parents (and by extension, the State of Florida), felt I should attend elementary school. I was very much against this for I enjoyed uninterrupted hours playing with my Fort Apache play set and curating my Matchbox car collection.

Lined up in an outdoor hallway, we marched down that gang plank to the classroom and our assigned seats. There, SHE appeared. SHE was Mrs. Creasy, who I then pegged at 123 years of age (she was 40 tops.) More importantly, SHE was not my mother. SHE was suddenly on a first-name basis and calling me Robbie.

Then came the Russians. I knew the Russians were coming because we were taught the duck-and-cover drill. By crouching under a thread-bare piece of wood masquerading as a desktop we would survive a nuclear strike launched some 90 miles south of us in Cuba. I looked up at the under-belly of my desk and discovered wads of gum—Communist-repelling gum, no doubt.

Safe for one day from the Russians, there was more chit-chat from Mrs. Creasy, some idle threat of learning how to write or read or some nonsense. Came then nap time, which was earlier than my nap time at home (then and now I take napping seriously). And I don't know if it was the Russian threat or the arbitrary napping sequence, but that's when Rusty lost it.

Rusty lived across the street from me and also felt his presence in first grade was not required. Unlike me, however, Rusty possessed a restlessness, a *daring* if you will. I figured I might as well stick out at least one day in school before alerting my parents I would be resuming my life exclusively on the home front. Rusty couldn't wait.

During nap time, he bolted for an open window (our school windows were kept open because air-conditioning wasn't available then). I saw Rusty's feral, scrawny backside wiggling through the window and toward a pasture of freedom. I saw Mrs. Creasy, whose nimbleness we underestimated, dart to the window and pry Rusty from his escape tunnel. He resisted. There were tears. She calmly yet firmly placed Rusty on his sleep mat.

I'd like to think no one napped that first school day in Mrs. Creasy's class. But we all slept like babies until it was snack time and soon our mothers came to pick us up from school. The Russians never came, and Rusty never escaped.

We were going to be all right.

Middle school dance

October 17, 2001

As a chaperone at Ridgely Middle School's dance, your first post is the cafeteria's lob- by. You stamp 200 hands, while making the predictable observation: The girls look much older, much more mature (although "mature" is too mature a word) than the boys. Maybe it's the tube-tops or the makeup or their height or the way the girls look you straight in the eye and you better stamp their hand pronto because they have places to go.

Many head for the cafeteria's dance floor. Rules state "no hugging, kissing, lap sitting or very physical dance styles, such as moshing or break dancing." The parents form an insecure perimeter, as the kids hop and slide but not mosh. The children, born in the late 1980s, sing along to Van Morrison's "Brown Eyed Girl." Hey where did we go, Days when the rains came, down in the hollow, playing a new game.

In the gym, mondo basketball is the game. Chaperones scramble to enforce the "balls-must-be-used-in-a-responsible-manner, no-'bomb,' " rule. A few wild half-court shots are permitted, though. Your kid jukes by, all sweaty and money-grubbing, and you swear he gives you a molecule of a smile. You are wonderfully distracted. No one is throwing any bombs. No one has uttered the word "anthrax."

You run into a friend of a friend. You and she watch for "unnecessary horseplay" in the gym, but your hearts aren't in the job. Remember Molly? Of course, you say. She was a lifeguard at your pool, maybe even babysat your babies once or twice. The girl (a woman now) moved to New York and worked at the World Trade Center. Molly was working there Sept. 11, but managed to escape. Oh, God, you say.

Another chaperone tells you to go into the bathroom, where a boy is seeking refuge from a pack of girls wearing makeup. They hang outside the bathroom door, waiting to haul him away. You tell the cowering kid he's one lucky boy. You tell him it's safe to come out of his hollow. Come out and play.

[7]

Memories From the Sunshine State

First Person: Yes, but does Maryland have mermaids?

July 28, 2013

I don't want to spark a Maryland-Florida rivalry since there is nothing to spark.

The fact is, pound-for-tacky-pound, my home state of Florida is the kitsch king of the roadside attractions. Maryland has its museums and theme parks, but for sheer sponge-diving, gator-wrasslin', aqua joy, the Sunshine State shamelessly leads the union.

By the late 19th century, tourists started seeping into Florida, traveling its highways (pre-interstate) and becoming easy marks for dyed-orange oranges (Indian River citrus!), glass-bottom boat rides, and gators of any size, age or infirmity.

Florida's first tourist was Juan Ponce de Leon (some young Spanish dude), whose presence gave birth to Florida's first roadside attraction, "The Fountain of Youth" in St. Augustine. Its guest book has signatures from 1867.

Besides gators and oranges, Floridians soon developed a thirst for oceanariums, shell shops, and, oh my yes, mermaids. A recent *New York Times* magazine piece reminded me of the mermaids of Weeki Wachee Springs in central Florida. The bubble-blowing ladies of the deep still perform their water ballet daily. And the theater still looks mostly empty.

On any kid's wishlist were also bumpy car or bus rides to the Miami Serpentarium, Silver Springs, Cypress Gardens, and a jungle of jungles—from Jungleland Snake Park, Gator Jungle and Jungle Adventures (featuring the largest man-made gator!) to Parrot Jungle and Monkey Jungle. Big fish tanks also sprang up: Marineland, Miami Seaquarium and its slow cousin, Ocean World.

I was a Seaquarium boy, where I saw Flipper (spoiler alert: there were multiple "Flippers" used on the TV show) and the famous albino porpoise, Carolina Snowball. I remember putting a quarter into some machine that made souvenir wax dolphins. I miss my wax dolphin. My brother preferred the Miami Serpentarium to see the venom maestro Bill Haast, handle—and often get bit by—rattlers, cobras and mambas. Haast lived to be 100.

In my 20 years in Maryland, I have seen the boondoggle that is Noah's Ark off the highway in Frostburg—forever incomplete, forever a monument to the patron saint of ministerial egoism. There's the Muffler Man statue in Havre de Grace, and Edgar Allan Poe's cryptic grave in Baltimore. I've even seen the hairspray tributes at the Towson grave of Divine—of John Waters fame.

But does Maryland have a Screamin' Gator Zip Line? A Skunk Ape Research Center? A cemetery that boasts a tombstone that says "I Told You I Was Sick"?

From what I've been told, Maryland had something called The Enchanted Forest. Grown Marylanders swoon at its mention to this day.

Opened in 1955, the fairy tale theme park was in Ellicott City off U.S. Route 40. Thousands of kids enjoyed "the Alice in Wonderland ride with teacup-shaped cars, a Cinderella's castle ride with mice for the cars, the "Little Toot" boat that took children to Mount Vesuvius for giant slides, and the Jungleland Safari which was driven by open Land Rover-type vehicles," says Wikipedia. For a while, this was pre-Disney World, mind you.

There must be other memorable Maryland attractions—roadside, seaside or otherwise. Please pass along any photos, comments, stories about the places you loved visiting when you were young or still visit.

If they involve mermaids, I'm so there.

Growing up means understanding hate in Dixie and the Sunshine State

September 3, 2017

Is there a statute of limitations on childhood naivete? On adult un-education?

The country continues to question its past and present in this time of statute and monument removal and confederacies of violent dunces. From the downed Roger B. Taney statue in Annapolis to the dropped playing of "Maryland, My Maryland" at University of Maryland football games, people are gut-checking their beliefs, customs and traditions.

Some are even discovering their hometowns for the first time.

In the 1960s, I was a child growing up in south Florida. I was taken to Fort Lauderdale beach before I could even swim. If there was unrest elsewhere in the country, it surely didn't happen on unspoiled Fort Lauderdale beach. Little did I know or learn in school.

In 1961, there was a series of "wade-ins "by black residents on the all-white beach at Las Olas Boulevard in Fort Lauderdale. A year before, my beach had been immortalized and romanticized in the popular beach movie, "Where the Boys Are." There weren't any black beachgoers in the movie, either.

Organized by the local NAACP, the wade-in participants—tired of trudging to the "blacks-only" sand scrap south of the "good" beach—were greeted by threats of police arrest and crowds of whites brandishing bottles and bats. The number of black participants increased, and eventually, a Broward Circuit judge allowed the protests to continue. Broward County's beaches were, from then on, desegregated.

I had no idea when and how this happened until I was at the beach a few years ago and noticed a historic marker chronicling the wade-ins. Don't know how long it has been there, but the marker wasn't erected in my time in south Florida. And I certainly didn't learn anything about segregated Florida beaches in my Florida classrooms (wishing to uphold school segregation, the Florida Legislature in 1957 opposed *Brown v. Board of Education*).

I never knew an NAACP pioneer named Harry T. Moore up the road in Brevard County, in a little Florida town called Mims, was killed along with his wife. KKK members planted and detonated a bomb under the floor boards of their home Christmas night, 1951. The Moores are considered the first NAACP members killed for civil rights activism. Their home was bombed on their 25th wedding anniversary. I learned about the Moores when I had the chance years later in Maryland to interview their daughter, Evangeline, who happened to be away from home that Christmas. She survived to tell her parents' story.

I didn't learn about Rosewood in school, either. In January 1923, black residents in the black town of Rosewood in Levy County, Florida, were nothing short of massacred by white vigilantes, some of whom had been deputized by the local sheriff. Parts of Florida were a Klan hot bed in the 1920s, when the hate group's membership reportedly peaked in the South. First I heard of the town's scorching was seeing John Singleton's movie "Rosewood" in 1997.

Then there was Reuben Stacy. I have relatives who still live in Davie, just west of where I grew up. It was a cow town then, sort of still is. It was also a Klan town. In 1935 (when my father was 10 and growing up in Fort Lauderdale), a 37-year-old black man named Reuben Stacy was shot and then hanged from a tree on Old Davie Road in Fort Lauderdale. The grisly photograph, which survived, is a rare visual account of a lynching in Florida.

A report from the nonprofit Equal Justice Initiative about lynchings across the South taught me something else. The Sunshine State ranked fifth among 12 states analyzed for the number of lynchings between 1877 and 1950. There were 331 lynchings in Florida and per capita, the state lynched people at a higher rate than any other, according to the group's findings. Maryland had 28.

In my naivete, I never thought of Fort Lauderdale as the South or me a Southerner (my mother was born in Chicago; my father's people were from North Dakota). Yes, we would drive on Dixie Highway, our main road, and shop at Winn-Dixie, our main grocery store, and play on the white beach sand of where the boys were all the while unaware of any wade-in as we waded in.

Once or twice I ate at our local Sambo's. That's right, Sambo's, where the restaurant chain's mascot was indeed a dark-skinned boy. Sambo's went bankrupt and sold its Fort Lauderdale location to Denny's. That was 1983.

But Southerners? Us? Naw.

By the way, Old Dixie Highway up the road in Riviera Beach from my old home isn't called Old Dixie Highway anymore. In 2015 the mayor and others, believing "Dixie" to be symbolic of racism, cross burnings and the Klan, re-named their section of the highway in honor of former president Barack Obama.

I also learned that from a newspaper article.

Little did I know.

Locking up a fast piece of your past

March 5, 2017

What was your favorite childhood bike?

Breaking news: My bike was stolen 42 years ago.

I came out of high school one day that year, and there was nothing but a severed bike chain where my yellow, Schwinn Varsity had been faithfully stowed. Suddenly, my wheels were gone. My gazelle-like 10-speed had been heisted while I was probably studying history and the back of a certain girl's head. She sat in front of me and the back of her head often distracted me from my studies.

The point is I want my bike back.

True I can't use it. My neighborhood has no sidewalks and roads both narrow and harrowing—most bike-unfriendly. When my kids were young and I was buying many bikes for them, I had to drive them well out of our neighborhood to teach them how to bike (I know, I know: poor us). Driving to bike felt ironic. Certainly not the spontaneous, convenient rite of passage I dreamed of in my quaint parent dreams. My kids seemed to learn driving sooner and better than they did biking.

In my day we loved our bikes, which were often stolen. *In my day*, we swore to ourselves, God and country we would never listen to anyone who started a sentence with *in my day*. Now here we are: bike-less grown-ups talking about our childhood bikes.

Come on, though, a Schwinn Varsity! The Mercedes Benz of bikes back then. If I could, I would thank my parents again for coughing up the dough to buy me that bike. I never took advantage of all 10 speeds given the pancake terrain of South Florida and the uselessness of upper gears. Our biggest hill was an ant hill. But me and buddies would caravan to Ft. Lauderdale beach on our 10-speeds. If it wasn't the best of times, it'll do and did.

But my bike got stolen at school. I had locked it and everything but learned that day the mean power of bolt cutters. A First World problem, granted. In no time, there followed cars and graduation and marriage and children and more bikes and cars and graduations *in their day*.

Then something happened last week.

I was on foot patrol at City Dock, my usual prowling and meandering engineered to get me lost for an hour. I walked along Dock Street, noting the returning and familiar boats in Ego Alley, when I passed Mission BBQ where Stevens Hardware used to be. On the sidewalk outside the storefront was a yellow, Schwinn Varsity 10-speed. It looked exactly like my year and model. It was beautiful.

Naturally, I wanted to take her for a spin. But inquiring inside as to the bike's owner and any potential lending seemed not only forward of me but generally frowned upon by the restaurant industry. As if in a trance, I did place my hands on the curled, taped handles and gazed upon the two gear shifts on this private property. The bike had a metal cup holder, an accessory long after my biking time.

I started walking back to my car when I turned back for a last look. It wasn't my old bike, of course. But the Schwinn Varsity 10-speed was a surprising and welcome stand-in. This bike, too, could go places. This bike, too, could speed strong-legged teenagers to a beach and be back tan and tired all before dinner. This bike, too, could get swiped. Because I didn't see a lock on the 10-speed on Dock Street.

In my day, we locked our bikes, which were stolen, in my day.

When prom backfires

May 18, 2014

Back when I was a kid we didn't have proms.

Naw, that isn't true. We had proms—we just didn't have 14-seat Lincoln Navigators, hot air balloons, cruise liners, gondolas, horse-drawn carriages or Sherpas to take us to prom.

I had my dad's 1974 Toronado.

Let me tell you about the 1974 Oldsmobile Toronado. The car had been Noah's first choice of transportation, but he opted for the smaller ark. Supposedly the first front-wheel drive car produced in America, the Toronado was a two-door coupe with a 455 cubic-inch Rocket V8. It was big and fast and mine for that May night in 1977.

It was also the first and only time I drove the Toronado.

It was also my first date—the girl I took to prom.

Imagine your first date with your father's car and a girl all in the same night? That's nerve-wracking. How nervous can you be sitting in the back of a limo that looks like the inside of a strip club? What's the worst that can happen? The sky roof doesn't open?

Anyway, I was behind the wheel of my dad's Toronado hurtling up 1-95 from Ft. Lauderdale to West Palm Beach. With a 455 cubic inch Rocket V8. With a girl. Up to that moment, my life had not provided remotely similar thrills.

The car handled beautifully. I was, however, stunned to look down at the speedometer and see I was going 88 mph. It felt like 28 mph. Being a responsible young adult and weeks away from graduation and soon an exciting future in journalism, I slowed the Toronado down to a safe 83 mph.

Along with my super-groovy mustache, my tuxedo made me look like a failed wedding singer. My date wore something beige or peach-colored or maybe it was blue. All I know is she looked a whole bunch different than she did just the Friday before in sixth-period English.

It was the smoothest ride of my life ... until I got cocky.

I wish I could remember how I introduced a really bad idea into what was shaping up to be a swell evening. It probably went a little something like this:

"I wonder what happens if I shift the car into reverse."

I don't remember how my date reacted. I imagine she was stunned, perhaps terrified, perhaps even suggested to me I not put my dad's Toronado into reverse given we were traveling at 83 mph.

You know that inner voice that tells us if we are doing something stupid? I had given my inner voice the night off with pay.

Now, I've heard haunting, terrifying sounds (most recently coming from a friend describing a kidney stone extraction), but I still haven't heard a sound as heart-stopping as that of a Toronado when jacked into reverse at high speeds. The sound started low under my feet, an earthquake of pain, followed by a rattling that I feared would reduce my dad's car to Lego bits.

I came to my senses and jammed the gear shift back down to drive. Miraculously, the Tornado also came to its senses. I feared I had killed my dad's car (and who wants *that* on their young resume), but the car was fine. My date and I drove in silence to our prom. I don't think I went over 45 mph.

So, what valuable lesson can I pass along to today's prom-goers?

If you give your inner voice the night off, please rush back home and make him tag along with you. He's not loads of fun, but he might save you from throwing your prom into painful, haunting reverse.

On this date in history

November 17, 2013

It was going to be a great day, maybe the greatest.

I was going to my first fast-food restaurant, the first fast-food restaurant in our South Florida town. A Burger King. Drive-through only. I had my order ready and everything. Hamburger and a vanilla shake. Best day of my life. Coming right up.

It was around 1:30 when we headed from our home to the Burger King. We were in my mother's Mercury. Copper colored, I think. Power windows, I know. I played with the power windows until I was told I could catch my neck in the window. I stopped playing with the power windows.

My mother was driving. My grandmother was in the passenger side. I was in the back.

I was 4.

This was a special treat not only because we were going to our first fast-food restaurant but because my grandmother was with us. I was with my two favorite people in the world.

We pulled up to the window. A girl—a woman—same thing to me back then—stuck her head out. My mother leaned her head out of the window. Both heads leaning toward one another. I wasn't sure, but I guessed she was taking our orders. I waited my turn to order my hamburger and vanilla shake.

I waited. But no one took my order, and I had practiced and everything.

The girl and my mother kept talking, but their voices were so soft. Then I saw my mother talk to my grandmother, but again so softly I couldn't hear a word they were saying. Grown-up talk, I figured. I just wanted my fast food. Could I eat it in the car? We were *never* allowed to eat in the car, but maybe this one time?

After they talked, I saw my mom sag in her front seat as if something heavy had struck her. She looked like she would fall, but thankfully she was sitting. I looked at my grandmother. She didn't look like she was falling. She put her hand on her daughter's shoulder as if to also brace her from some impossible fall.

I looked at the girl in the drive-through window. She was crying. I wondered if my mom was crying. I looked at her. I saw her straighten up in the front seat. She started the Mercury, and we went back home. I never got my hamburger and vanilla shake.

Last weekend I went home to visit my mother. In the family room there's a bookcase where she keeps old newspaper clippings and *Life* magazines. My mother, a lifelong Democrat and Catholic, saved so many articles and photographs about the assassination of her president 50 years ago this week.

During my visit, we talked about the family, my job, her yard, the lowly Miami Dolphins and a songbird she inherited from her granddaughter. The night before I left I mentioned the approaching anniversary. I reminded her of us being at the Burger King, how Grandma was with us, what I planned to order, how the food never came.

My mother seemed to sag again, so I stopped talking about her president.

Paul is still not dead

February 9, 2014

The very true and very unofficial history of the Beatles on the 50th anniversary of their American live television debut:

Feb. 9, 1964.

It's time. Come on, come on. Turn on Ed Sullivan.

We gather around the TV set—a black Zenith the size of a freight car.

Ed Sullivan's gigantic head appears. Amid carnal screams, he introduces the Fab Four. Ed's head frightens me for I am young (I turned 5 seven hours earlier.)

The boys from Liverpool sing.

"All My Loving."

"She Loves You."

My brother, sisters and I are in trance. My father is not impressed. These guys aren't Duke Ellington or Louis Armstrong.

"I Want to Hold your Hand."

"'Til There Was You."

All the other acts taped their appearances so not to compete with the screaming. We don't scream in our house, so there's no competition here, either.

"I Saw Her Standing There."

A light goes on in my normal-sized head.

So, *this* is music.

1967.

I ask Santa to buy me the Beatles' "Magical Mystery Tour." "Penny Lane," "Strawberry Fields Forever," "Fool on the Hill," "I Am the Walrus," etc.

On Christmas morning, there is no Beatles album. Santa, in the cruel guise of my mother, buys me the latest album by the American singing trio, The Lettermen. For those unfamiliar with The Lettermen, they do not share similar musical, personal or cultural stylings with the Beatles.

The Lettermen, in their wholesome sweaters, have a hit with "Goin' out of my Head." Meanwhile, in another universe, John Lennon *is* out of his head.

Semolina pilchard, climbing up the Eiffel Tower
Elementary penguin singing Hare Krishna
Man, you should have seen them kicking Edgar Allan Poe
I am the eggman. They are the eggmen.
I am the walrus ...

1968.

My best friend calls me into an emergency meeting in a closet in his house.

He just heard a song called "Lady Madonna." The lyrics, he claims, are dirty. This could be a game-changer.

In the darkness, he recites:

Lady Madonna, baby at your breast, wonder how you manage to feed the rest...

"Breast" sends us into a new, frightening, orbit. That something or someone could be at her breast. What are the implications of this!!??

We ponder the question in the closet until I have to go home for dinner. The next day, meeting in open, we conclude "Lady Madonna" is the greatest song ever.

1969.

A rap on my bedroom window.

Urgent news from same friend.

A bulletin has reached us in South Florida all the way from London. Paul is dead.

"What are you talking about?"

My friend tells me there are clues on their album covers and songs. Just listen to the end of "Strawberry Fields Forever" when John clearly mumbles "I bury Paul."

I can't confirm this because Santa got me a Lettermen album, but I believe my friend.

In the morning I alert my older brother. He has every Beatles album. He can confirm the news of Paul's tragic passing.

In a style unique to older brothers, my brother not only conveys the depth of the rumor's inaccuracy but also signals that perhaps a restraining order would best keep me away from him.

1970.

Yoko Ono.

And the name shall never be spoken again.

1980.

The Dakota. Mark David Chapman. "The Catcher in the Rye." The day the music died. Imagine there's no heaven.

We bury John.

Feb. 9, 2014.

It's on. Come on, come on. Turn on your laptop.

The Beatles' first appearance on Ed Sullivan is on YouTube.

Ed's scary head appears. Amid carnal screaming, he introduces the boys from Liverpool.

She was just 17
And you know what I mean
And the way she looked
Was way beyond compare...

A light goes on again.

Memories of working as an extra on the less-than-classic 'Jaws 3-D'

June 9, 2013

Not to question the public's taste in movies, but I need to question the public's taste in movies.

I see you jamming theaters to see this summer's blockbusters—namely, sequels to "Fast and Furious," "Star Trek," "Iron Man" and "The Hangover." Millions and millions spent on what? Entertaining, thrilling, funny movies?

Why?

Why, when in the comfort of your own home entertainment system you can stumble almost any week on the greatest movie sequel of our lifetime. While others might quibble and claim "The Godfather Part 11" holds that honor, this is no time for quibbling.

This is time for action.

This is time for "Jaws 3-D."

This second sequel to Steven Spielberg's 1975 "Jaws"—considered the first summer "blockbuster"—is a cinematic tour de force that when released in 1983, forever neutered the phrase "tour de force."

If you don't know, "Jaws 3-D" is the story of a killer mommy shark terrorizing water skiers and the heavily tanned in an Orlando, Fla., theme park. In the end, the shark dies from a grenade in its throat. Other stuff happens involving blood and bobbing heads and water skier pyramids. But the key plot point is the grenade-in-the-shark-mouth trick.

The movie was directed by none other than the production designer for the first "Jaws"—and by none other, I mean I don't know his name. The movie starred a young Dennis Quaid as Mike Brody, son of Sheriff Brody. Baltimore's Bess Armstrong and Louis Gossett Jr. rounded out the cast, as did talented, selfless extras who were hired during filming at Orlando's SeaWorld 30 years ago.

Reviewers, while sparing the extras, savaged the movie.

"Surprisingly tepid."

"Enough is too much—even in 3-D. The franchise stinks."

"I have no respect for this film."

Came the reviews on the online movie site, Rotten Tomatoes, which added its own 12-percent "rotten" rating.

What went wrong? Some say the producers should have stuck with the original idea of hiring "National Lampoon's" John Hughes (he of "The Breakfast Club" and "Uncle Buck) to write a spoof called "Jaws 3, People 0." But that idea was canned. Cooler, less-fun heads prevailed, and the "Jaws" brand was maintained and by that I mean maimed.

Would it have been a better comedy? Of course.

But let's focus on what went so very right with "Jaws 3-D."

Me.

For reasons best left unexplored, I found myself in Orlando in 1983 and standing in line to work a week as a movie extra. I got $50 a day and free lunch. I got to leer at Bess Armstrong, who did not return my leers. I got to chat up Dennis Quaid in between "set-ups," which is movie talk for waiting around for hours while stuff is set up then set up all over again and life's precious moments tick away.

During one set-up, Dennis and I discussed the craft of acting:

"How you doing?" I said.

"Good."

We both watched a man load a golf cart with popcorn for our scene.

"So, do you like acting?" I said.

And Dennis said something I still think about every day.

"It beats tarring roofs."

Then the camera rolled. All acting is reacting, as any extra knows. And my reaction to shark-spooked Mike Brody racing toward me in his popcorn-packed golf cart—mere seconds of screen time—is nothing short of somnambulant. In fact, I might have been sleep walking.

It's eerie to see yourself preserved on film from 30 years ago. I was reed thin. Had the Polo tucked in, for some reason. And my hair color was that of any Florida boy looking for summer work and without a clue what his own sequel would be.

I just hoped it would beat tarring roofs.

First Person: My own personal Roswell

July 14, 2013

ROSWELL (AP)—Google is marking the 66th anniversary of a New Mexico newspaper's report of a captured "flying saucer" with an interactive Doodle.

Well, that's all interactive and cool, but for those who have encountered UFOs, no Doodle can erase the lifelong effects of these close encounters.

For fear of certain inalienable rights being stripped from me by anti-UFO government forces, I've always kept silent about my brushes with aliens.

Until now.

On the 66th anniversary of Roswell, I feel compelled to share three official cases in the hopes they will inspire others to come forward, because you're not alone.

None of us are.

General Sightings Case No. 1:

I must have been around 4. I vaguely remember climbing aboard a vehicle that sped away at high speeds to a place I'd never been. Once there, I was brought to a small room with four chairs and what UFO field investigators later identified as a Formica kitchen table.

This is difficult to talk about even now, but I was forced to drink a strange beverage as two, white creatures hovered over me. They smelled of talc and cough drops. I was petrified—plus, the beverage was not tasty at all.

Days later when I mentioned the event to my parents, they told me my first visit to my grandparents' home had not gone particularly well. Seized by a health kick, they had offered me carrot juice. Moments later, I had placed a call to my parents seeking immediate retrieval.

To this day, I avoid carrot juice.

General Sightings Case No. 2:

I must have been around 13. My buddy Lewis and I were fishing in the Everglades. It was just after dusk. The South Florida sky was illuminated with stars. We anchored our Jon boat in the sawgrass. Around us, nothing but sky and water and the sounds of nature. We were the only people in the universe.

So we thought.

I laid back in the boat and closed my eyes. Sleep eluded me on account it was 6:45 p.m. So, I gazed upon the darkening sky when, to my horror, I saw a bright orange, crinkly UFO streak across the sky. Was it St. Elmo's Fire? (You know, the Sesame Street puppet.) A weather balloon? Some lost kite?

I closed my eyes in the hopes I was dreaming. But when I opened my eyes again, another orange UFO streaked literally inches from my head. I turned to ask Lewis if he had seen it, but he was busy flinging Cheetos at me. I never asked him why because it didn't seem relevant considering we were under invasion.

General Sightings Case No. 3:

I must have been around 50 when my last encounter occurred. Again, it's painful to share and certainly was painful to experience. First, I was taken to Baltimore and drugged—possibly with carrot juice—and placed in a strange bed surrounded by little green men and women who put tubes and needles in me. They made me say my name over and over again. At first, I resisted.

"I'm Charles Dickens."

"I'm Atticus Finch."

"Kareem Abdul-Jabbar?"

But they broke me, and I gave up my name. I was wheeled to another room with more little green men and women. There were blinding overhead lights, which must have been their spaceship. Then, from the corner of my eye, I saw it. A long, unidentified, hose-like creature with a camera for a face. It was horrifying. It came closer to be, embarrassingly close...

...then I don't remember anything else because I lost consciousness. When I awoke, I was back in a strange bed and still wearing non-human clothing since the back opened too freely. The little green men and women re-appeared at my bedside.

This next part is equally foggy, but they claimed what I saw was a common medical instrument that is quite safe and potentially could save my life. But that's what aliens always say.

To this day, I avoid colonoscopies.

[8]
Call of the
Wild

Osprey Cam Update: Audrey preens; Tom still a no-show

March 18, 2015

Tom and Audrey, "The Chesapeake's favorite osprey couple," are back on their top secret Kent Island platform.

Well, we think Tom is back.

For years, the osprey couple has been observed on a camera posted atop the homey platform. The nonprofit Chesapeake Conservancy, which runs the osprey cam, reports the osprey couple recently returned from their winter migration in South America. The platform is nest-free—for the time being. Monday afternoon, Audrey (we think it was Audrey) was seen standing guard over a severed fish tail. At the time, Tom was nowhere to be seen. We imagine his return...

Audrey: So, Tom my love, my sweet, my ruffled dumpling, where have you been?

Tom: Just took a stroll around the old neighborhood.

Audrey: Without me? We spent the whole winter apart—me in French Guiana, you in Venezuela doing God-knows-what. We finally get back into town, and you take off already?

Tom: Don't take it personally, sugar beak.

Audrey: Well, my sweet bird cakes, I've been standing here looking at a bare platform. Remember the whole nesting thing?

Tom: But we don't, uh, get together, for awhile yet. Isn't a nest a little premature?

Audrey: Not for a bird man with such strong, mighty talons...

Tom: But my svelte winged darling, I need, you know, a little rest. We just flew in from South America. Have some mercy.

Audrey: (Trying not to look hurt) All right, I understand.

Tom: Plus, it's March Madness and I'm late doing my brackets.

Audrey: So, that's where you have been all day! Making your cute little brackets!!!!! You didn't stop to bring back a single twig! And all I'm stuck with is a bloody fish tail.

Tom: If you give me a chance, I can find the head if you want. It's the best part, after all.

Audrey: No, Tom, I don't want a bloody fish head. I want to nest.

Tom: We will, I promise. Don't we every year?

Audrey: It just feels different this year. You feel different.

Tom: No, it's just...it's just...Kentucky, darling. They haunt me.

Audrey: (Readies herself to fly off platform) I need to get some air, Tom.

Tom: Honey darling sweet beak?

Audrey: What?

Tom: If you think of it, can you bring back some twigs?

Tuesday Update:

11:30 a.m.:

While staring hypnotically at the osprey cam today, I noticed the presence of a half dozen sticks on the platform.

The ancient work has begun.

4:30 p.m.:

I'm not going to make a habit of this, I'm not going to make a habit of this, I'm not going to...

I think I'm looking at Audrey because the female osprey typically arranges the twigs for the nest. And Audrey is fussing and kerfuffling with Tom's initial handiwork. (It's true what they say about their nests; these birds will use plastic bags, tinsel, boat line, about anything to make a home. So far, it looks like Tom's and Audrey's home will also feature non-organic elements.)

I still haven't seen the two of them together. But I am not worried. I believe in them.

And I need to stop watching at least until tomorrow.

Because there's both a certain tranquility and madness to this pastime, and the line is starting to blur...

Wednesday Update:

5 p.m.:

Still no sign of Tom.

Audrey was seen checking out the starter nest, which doesn't appear to have been worked on at all today. I tried to read her mood, but she kept her back to me.

Somehow *I* feel responsible for today's lack of progress.

In a programming note, the osprey cam was temporarily down this morning. Something about an outage of Atlantic Broadband in the region.

Tom?

A mammal only a mother (and father) mammal could love

July 19, 2105

Are you looking to adopt a pet? Think sea cow.

"A manatee has been spotted in the Bay. Help us keep these animals safe"

Tweet from National Aquarium in Baltimore

Few things make this Florida Boy's heart jerk more than a manatee sighting.

No matter what I do, where I work, where I live, I am never far in my head from the water. In Anne Arundel County, I'm pretty far from the water or at least access to it. *The Capital's* Rema Rahman begins her 3-part project today on the lack of public water access. Our recreational, environmental and economic bond with water is perpetual. As is news from the water—tragic speedboat races in Kent Narrows, near-routine boating accidents and rescues, general threatened marine life, specific cownose ray clubbings and for fun, kayaking, paddle boarding and, of course, sailing.

And if we are lucky, a manatee sighting.

Manatees, mostly known in southern waters, occasionally lumber into the Bay. Remember Chessie? A sort of Halley's Manatee, Chessie swam up into Maryland's warm summer waters a few times over 17 years. He was a rock star—with 22 boat scars on his back. Propeller and other collision scars are often the wounds on the some 4,800 Florida manatees that remain. The population's senior statesman is Snooty, a 67-year-old manatee living in Bradenton, FL.

A relative of the elephant, the endangered manatee is a mammal only a mother (and father) mammal could love. It has thick, wrinkled skin, no outer ears, a prehensile upper lip, tiny little eyes, and tiny little hairs over its grayish brown hide. It swims slowly, sometimes barrel rolling for kicks. Its breath is probably not tops. Its figure is not svelte unless you consider Kim Kardashian's backside petite.

This past week's sighting was in Charles County, where a manatee was grazing and snuffling about off the Potomac River. Naturally, I follow the news of any manatee, but my heart belongs to one.

Squeaky.

Squeaky is a 4-year-old, West Indian manatee living at Blue Spring State Park in Central Florida. This past Father's Day, I became Squeaky's adoptive parent thanks to my daughter who gifted me the adoption. I've never been one to join a club, but I believe I'm now a member of the Save the Manatee Club. My "Certificate of Adoption" features a grainy picture of Squeaky with her mother Amber. My certificate is signed by Jimmy Buffett, so yeah, I'm kind of a rock star, too.

My manatee's biography focuses mainly on Amber, who was abandoned by her mother and needed rescuing and care at SeaWorld. Fortunately, the popular theme park cannot make loads of money off killer manatee tricks, so Amber recuperated quietly backstage. Well-nursed, Amber returned to Blue Spring State Park in 2009.

Soon, Amber was pregnant but had a stillbirth in 2010. Amber visited the park again the following season.

"She was not observed to be pregnant," according to her bio.

In 2011, Amber stunned her keepers by giving birth to Squeaky. They left for the St. Johns River and returned a year later.

"Squeaky was soon frolicking everywhere. She was even discovered upside down, scratching her belly on the bottom of the research canoe!"

This I want to see.

As a member of the Save the Manatee Club and Jimmy Buffet-signed certificate holder, I have an open invitation to visit Blue Spring State Park in the winter. Water temps then are good for manatee visits.

I'm not sure what I'd say to Squeaky.

Hi?

Be safe?

Hi and be safe, rock star.

Quick! Spray that bat house!!!

May 15, 2018

Update: The bat pheromones via silver snazzy canister arrived via UPS person. The product is to be sprayed liberally at the entrance of the bat house. It was. Come forth bats. Your scented home awaits.

Holy white-nose syndrome!

Lately, I've been worried about white-nose syndrome. I've also been worrying about the complete human experience, but one must narrow the field to get any sort of writing done.

White-nose syndrome has become an overpowering disease wiping out more than 7 million bats in North America and targeting the common little brown bat. The condition is named for a fungus that grows around the muzzles and wings of hibernating bats. If that wasn't enough, pesticides and habitat destruction are also contributing the population decline.

I sound like a terrifically caring guy, but I had never heard about this or any bat syndrome when I took possession of the bat house.

One perk of having older children with jobs is the improved quality of parental gifts. The kids bought me a really nice bat house for my birthday—or maybe it was Christmas—I do not remember. I say "really nice bat house" without knowing what an average or below average bat house might look like. The literature (OK, a baby pamphlet) that came with the bat house says it took engineers 10 years to come up with the thing's design.

I'm no bat house engineer (just 120 college credits short!), but the block-of-wood-with-bat-meshing thing looks strikingly similar to every other bat house. But who am I to question 10 years of dedicated toil in the name of bat domiciles? The point is bats might be a bit safer and more secure in these treed boxes.

The instructions called for the bat house to be affixed to a dead tree with a southern sunny exposure and hung 12 to 15 feet above the ground. I have a few upright dead trees but not an accommodating ladder. The bat house is maybe 10 feet off the ground—I wasn't going to break my neck over it.

Bats can eat as many as 1,200 insects an hour, which sounds like a ridiculous typo. Twelve-hundred insects an hour doesn't leave a lot of time for goofing off or watching something on HBO. And I want to meet the person who tallied some bat's hourly chow. But I would insist on meeting at a public place during the day with witnesses and preferably pepper spray.

"As consumers of vast numbers of pests, bats rank among humanity's most valuable allies," so offers the pamphlet.

Wanted: willing tenants.

In this neck of the country's woods, the little brown bat (*Myotis lucifugus* or, literally, "My Lord I'm Cuter than I Look") is common. Bats have made their way into my home over the years—you haven't lived until a bat dive-bombs your second-grader in the family room.

The challenge is to lure bats into *their* house.

"You can expect the bat house to become occupied within a year to three years."

Three years? You took 10 years to build this thing, and you're telling me I might have to wait three years to see if it works?

No, no, no. This batman doesn't do waiting.

Which brings me to another perk of having kids with jobs—their gifts can come with a Part 2. And Part 2 of my bat house present is a forthcoming batch of bat pheromones. Normally I would leave such an intimate subject to participating boy and girl bats. But I'm not waiting three years.

I want bats. I want action.

Holy bat pheromones!!!

Enemies at the gate—deck, porch, soul

September 27, 2015

How much does a woodpecker peck when a woodpecker pecks wood?

I always knew my yard was plotting against me. That the moment I move, retire or escape, my yard and its inhabitants will take sole possession of my borrowed parcel.

It has been waiting for the day.

When my receding hairline of grass goes bald. When my buckled driveway concedes to a Trumpian takeover of weeds. When my ailing Chestnut oaks topple on my house freeing the soil once again to house the moles and mice so rudely displaced by a 1985 housing development.

When my side deck collapses under the supervision of a single woodpecker who will remain nameless.

But I know who is he.

And I know what he wants.

I first heard signs of trouble when I was awakened summer mornings by the sound of rapping. With grown children still at home, I assumed one of them had decided to remodel the basement to their own extracurricular specifications. The sound sounded like someone or something was deliberately, rhythmically dismantling the property. I queried my children, but their alibis proved sound.

Next, I wondered if squirrels were to blame. One chewed my hammock to pieces, but I didn't think him capable of taking down a house because I still believe in the innate goodness of rodents. Stink bugs, when organized and really ticked off, have been known to ruin property, relationships and weaker nations. But I haven't seen any this year yet.

I was stumped—until last weekend.

Rapping resumed. Following the sound to the side deck, I saw a beady red head merrily pecking away at one of the two wood posts holding up the deck. (Disclaimer: I never use the side deck. Its purpose remains unclear—other than to break the fall of anyone walking out the door leading to the side deck that leads to the ground.) I sprung into action and I mean I first made coffee and played a bit with my dog Earle. The point is I sprung.

I stepped out onto my side deck, which sunk as if in quick sand. I stepped back into the house. I walked outside around the house where my trained homeowner's eyes spotted two fat toothpicks holding up my deck. The bite marks resembled more the work of beavers than a lone, garden-variety red-bellied woodpecker. He had pecked the wood almost down to the nails, and he wasn't done.

Did I somehow insult this woodpecker or his girlfriend?

Am I wrong to have a side deck?

Will a plastic owl, windsock or a blaring TV stop the invader?

Why doesn't he pick on one of my dead Chestnut oaks?

What's the optimum retirement age? 65, 67, 70, today?

I retreated to my porch on the *back* deck, a wonderful jetty where I spend much time in shallow, soothing thought. Here, no woodpecker, stink bug or dead oak bothers me. Only the sound of whistling cardinals, chipping chipmunks and crying hawks disturb—no, enrich!—my back-deck tranquillity.

Then came a new sound. Not rapping, but a faint scratching. I sprung into action again and walked around the back deck. There, three holes the sizes of gum balls in the wood. I pressed my ear to the holes and heard scratching then buzzing. From the holes emerged carpenter bees, busy at work gnawing the other end of my house.

I went inside to be with the dog.

He means no harm.

[9]

It's Actually About Me

Standing tall and hating gray

April 19, 2015

Last week in this space colleague Iris Krasnow issued a pro-gray hair manifesto that cannot go unchallenged.

Normally, I don't take sides of issues because that requires analyzing issues, and who has time for that? You know, with baseball season underway and all.

But her column unsettled me. Just listen to her opening words:

"Men are allowed to age gracefully..."

Stop right there, Iris Krasnow, colleague.

Despite all your book readin' and book writin,' you have clearly fallen for the oldest stereotype in post-modern American culture (and by "post-modern American culture" I mean I don't know what that means), which is: Men are allowed to old gracefully, i.e., as they get gray, grayer, and grayest until their hair resembles a sad, small dome of young snow, society both allows and rewards them.

Ha!

Yes, I said ha! With an exclamation mark! And onto thee I say ha! Again!!! Because you probably have a point there, but let's move on before I lose my fierce anti-gray momentum.

Let me tell you a story about a lad growing up in South Florida.

The boy started going gray *en utero*, a first in recorded medical history. The attending doctor told the boy's mother at the moment of birth, "Congratulations, Mrs. Hiaasen! You have a baby boy! A rather old-looking baby boy, but still!" That boy, who would fight Adolescent Gray Hair Discrimination, would also find relief in the carcinogenic Florida sun.

Years spent playing outside turned his premature-premature gray hair into golden blonde. Girls took notice. Questions were asked behind closed doors: Who is that blonde kid? What makes him tick? Is that his real hair color? How many *Chicago* albums does he own?

Thanks largely to advantages his blonde hair afforded him, that boy was able to matriculate from elementary to middle school. But during puberty ("The Dark Ages"), the boy's boyish blonde hair showed signs of rebellion. It curled. It waved. It became less blonde. But did he give up his dreams of matriculating to high school? He did not.

Then, in his late 20s, the temples of the man-child began to gray. His mother blamed the stress of work on her son's hair mutiny. No, the stress of work caused him to drink not go gray, he lovingly relayed to his mother. The culprit must be heredity. He looked to blame someone swinging from his family tree, but there were no guilty relations. Yes, two first cousins did marry way back then, but this troubling discovery was beside the point.

What can we say about the man in his 30s? Imagine Steve Martin, without the banjo or talent. A banjo-less, talent-less man gone gray way before his time. Where was colleague Iris Krasnow then in support gray hair?

Buckling under society's abject hatred of young male gray hairness, the banjo-less man slithered into a hair salon and asked that his hair be colored. Pestered by invasive questions like "What color are you aiming for?," the man closed his eyes and allowed the stylist to do whatever. She did whatever.

For weeks, the man walked through life with hair the color of a nice end table from Ikea. He did not look younger. He did not receive movie roles turned down by George Clooney. His hair frightened young children and other Ikea furniture. His mother didn't recognize him anymore. Worse, his defiled hair got very angry. When he failed to return to the stylist for repeated coloring, the man's hair turned shock-white.

It's been that shade ever since.

Women, colleague Iris Krasnow wrote last week, should embrace their gray hair (Men, I write, should embrace women's gray hair—but only if they know each really well). Women, stand tall and go gray. It's not a fashion statement; it's a statement you're comfortable with your age, she wrote.

All good words.

All lies!

I do not stand tall with my "Granny Hair," which remains an affront to my time-less, thriving vanity. I had to accept the fact I got gray embryonically early and I will never learn the banjo. But I do not have to accept the fact my hair is the color of premature death.

On a brighter note, I got my haircut the other week. I might have been whining about my hair color when the gal shampooing me said the nicest, most unsolicited thing.

"Well, at least you have hair."

And I felt young again—young and gray but growing old gracefully, finally.

When the moon is in the seventh—or second—house

February 5, 2017

Fellow Aquarians, don't bank on your horoscope

Stay the course, Aquarius. You might be at wit's end waiting for a deal to bear fruit, but don't quit five minutes before the miracle happens! Today's merger of the moon and Venus in your grounded second house reminds you that, however frustrating it can be, slow and steady WILL win the race. Irritated at someone who's thwarting your progress? Kill 'em with kindness. This can shift the energy and open up the floodgates. At work, you could finally get the recognition you deserve—and a hefty raise to go along with it." Horoscope for Aquarius, Elle magazine

Dear Horoscope,

Thank you for the kind pick-me-up. My birthday is this week and, as an avid Aquarius, I appreciate the good juju.

The heavens clearly care about me. So, I hope you don't mind if I press you for a few details. Generally, things are looking pretty swell for this old water-bearer boy. But I do seek specifics.

You refer to a certain deal on the verge of bearing fruit. "You might be at wit's end." I lost most of my wits around 1995. As for a fruit-bearing deal, I can't remember the last deal remotely involving me or any member of the fruit group.

I did receive a rather pointed needle shoved into the heel of my foot to ease my plantar fasciitis. That was one helluva deal—*"but don't quit five minutes before the miracle happens!"*

OK, I'll wait for my miracle before gnawing off my own heel.

You mention the moon and Venus merging in my second grounded house. That's interesting—in the way "interesting" is interchangeable with "incomprehensible." I reluctantly own a second home since my mother passed last year. And it's true I'm in weekly negotiations regarding contracts and prospective buyers and roof inspections and insulting counter offers. And it's extremely accurate to say my wits have ended.

But no moon or Venus has offered to have my back. *"However frustrating it can be, slow and steady WILL win the race."*

Yeah, let's see if this April closing happens.

Am I irritated at someone thwarting my progress? You bet. It's the same person thwarting my progress since I was born. He's just a little bit older this week. *"Kill 'em with kindness."* Agreed. I plan to order myself a gallon of Buffalo wings and stuff my face today as the Falcons upset the Patriots 34-31 in the Super Bowl.

"At work, you could finally get the recognition you deserve..."

Coincidentally, it's performance evaluation time. Time for those languid, restorative conversations—excuse me, *dialogues*—between you and your boss across a desk—*a power preferential*—where priorities and learning and development plans are crafted using only the boldest of action verbs. What follows are 3 or more stated improvement needs—*career stallers.*

Off the top of my head I can't think of any career stallers other than maybe reading your horoscope at work. That and delusional self-assessments masquerading as newspaper humor.

"...and a hefty raise to go along with it."

Oh thank you, wise and generous Horoscope.

Forever yours,

Wit's End

Dating is still too much pressure and heartache

September 13, 2015

And now for my next trick—lower blood pressure

Our date was in trouble from the start.

Yes, I had canceled on him last year. It's hard to build a relationship when you forget to call, much less see someone. I screwed up, OK? To make amends, I made sure I kept our date this year. I even wore a pressed dress shirt and shaved.

After exchanging clipped hellos, I was asked to step on one of those scales prizefighters use at weigh-in. I don't know about you, but I never like to begin a date by stepping on any scale.

"Insurance companies would consider you overweight," he said after awhile.

We hadn't seen each other in two years, and he tells me insurance companies would consider me overweight. He must think that, too! But he doesn't have the nerve to be brutally honest.

Instead, he said: "You're a few pounds heavier since the last time I saw you."

The last time I saw you. I caught that dig. He hasn't forgotten how I stood him up last year. Since I'm a better (and heavier) man, I took another tact.

"You look like you have lost weight," I told my doctor.

The old-reverse-compliment trick.

"About 20 pounds."

He talked about family history, stress, diet and exercise. He talked about not wanting me to have a heart attack. He talked about alcohol.

"How much wine are you drinking?"

Finally, a shard of hope. Maybe we were going to open a bottle of Pinot Noir. But this was not to be the direction our date took. He seriously wanted me to provide the number of glasses of wine I drink in a week. So, I did what you do on dates when things aren't going swimmingly.

I fibbed.

Undaunted, he proceeded to tell me—lecture me more like it!—on how alcohol consumption is a contributing factor to high blood pressure.

Of course I have high blood pressure. I was a nervous wreck seeing him again after so long. And why couldn't we have met at Chili's or Chick-Fil-A instead of some nondescript office building? Was he ashamed to be seen with me in public? Also, how does one truly measure the pressure of one's heart? Such a thing can't be quantified or given a number.

Yes, it can. Two sets of numbers. And mine are risky high and have been since our last date when he asked me to take my own blood pressure and chart and email him the results.

"I sent you a letter about that, but I guess ...." his voice, trailing.

Now I felt guilty, lazy, fat, alcoholic, near-death and hungry since I hadn't had a thing to eat or drink since the night before. I was saving my appetite in hopes of having that bottle of wine or maybe ducking out for lunch. Man, I read this man wrong. All I wanted to do was to end our date, which clearly wasn't going anywhere.

Not so fast.

As if I hadn't given enough of my heart, he wanted me to give blood (to analyze and ridicule no doubt!) First, he wanted me to slip into something more comfortable, although he didn't use *those* words.

Women have been known to recall childbirth as if we men are really to believe this holy, natural event is accompanied by alleged discomfort. Women have never been on our dates. In the name of decency—and there's a chance you might be having your breakfast—I will say that my date concluded with an intimate maneuver during which not a word was spoken nor wine opened.

When my national nightmare discreetly ended, we said our good-byes. Certain promises were again made. Talk of penciling in another date. A sincere pledge to keep a blood pressure chart.

Oh, dear heart.

How much pressure can you take?

Speaking of dachshund underwear

February 23, 2014

ADULT BRIEFS
Case of LG adult briefs $30 or best offer.
Sold!

No, wait.

Too many times I've jumped at tantalizing offers only to regret my impulse buying.

I'm not even a briefs kind of guy. I know this question secretly gnaws on the respectable minds of readers. I can't tell you how many times I'm stopped in the county and asked if I'm a boxers or briefs man—although, if pressed, I could put the number at zero. (Probably is beside the point to mention my priceless pair of Christmas boxers featuring antler-wearing dachshunds.)

But what if I underwent a revolutionary transformation and switched to briefs? What would that mean for my career and happiness? Would briefs lead to a promotion? Or hamper my ability to move freely when walking?

I wouldn't start with a case of them. That's too much of a commitment. I'd buy one, maybe two pairs. Try them on for size but not in front of the mirror because in 32 states—including Maryland—it's a felony for men over 50 to stare at themselves in the mirror while wearing briefs.

Maybe I'd take them out for a spin one day at work—see if I develop a swagger, see if I increase my confidence and decrease my day dreaming. Finally, I'd get that raise! I can hear it now:

"I speak for a few of us when I say we all have noticed your excellent work as of late. We don't know what's changed, but keep it up."

"I'm a changed man. I switched to briefs, and I'm feeling younger, leaner, hungrier, more primal, more—"

"OK, I think you can stop there. In closing, and to recognize your recent contributions to our company, we are giving you a raise."

"How much?"

"This is where it gets complicated due to our state-of-the-art accounting practices."

"How much?"

"Not much."

Capitalizing on this momentum, I'd start wearing briefs every day at work. Several pairs at a time; thus, doubling and tripling my chances of even greater advancement, riches and envy. I'd be invited to conduct journalism seminars and webinars on "The Power of the Briefs." The Pulitzer committee would take notice. But like other mavericks before me, my rise would be followed by a fall because of society's multi-brief bias:

"I speak for the entire organization when I say, are you wearing multiple undergarments?"

"Why, yes, I am. Is there a problem?"

"It's the waddling and tipping over when you try to stand. It upsets your co-workers."

"Is there a written policy against wearing five pairs of briefs?"

"Well, no."

"Is there a policy against waddling?"

"You're missing the point."

But people miss the point sometimes. Take the guy who writes about adult briefs only to discover that "adult briefs" are of the very personal and disposable kind and have nothing to do with the boxers vs. briefs discussion.

That guy missed the point.

Trash talking: Tales from the pit

August 30, 2015

What's the second best free fun?

I love the smell of garbage in the morning.

It hits the moment you pull off the main road, past the "No Scavenging" sign, and approach the citizen drop-off area in what they call in my neighborhood the Baltimore County Central Acceptance Facility.

The dump.

Which is a low-rent euphemism for a sanctuary of sorts. For some men, their kingdom is a golf course, Home Depot, bar, boat, church or man cave. For others, it's the dump. It's the moment when you back your vehicle into the citizen drop-off area, wiggle into your work gloves, move to the back of your vehicle, and start throwing junk over the wall and into the great pit.

Oh, the sounds of breaking glass, shattering wood, exploding lamps, all that purging.

Last Saturday morning I had a date with the dump. I was looking forward to it all week. But this time I would have something to show for myself. I always put too much pressure on bringing big-ticket items. Too often I pull up with offerings that I could easily put in a regular garbage can at home—but then where would I go Saturday mornings?

This time I had the mother lode:

A trampoline.

A hammock.

A rain barrel.

(The 20-year-old trampoline was a bittersweet passing—a rusty relic of my children's childhoods.)

(The hammock was sabotaged by a squirrel whose clandestine rope-nibbling led to my rapid free fall. The ground, turns out, is a very hard thing.)

(I forget to drain my rain barrels in the winter so the frozen water splits them open like melons. Melons are cheaper.)

So, I loaded up my Prius, drove out to Warren Road, turned off onto the dirt road, past the scrap metal, batteries, electronics and light bulbs stations, and down yonder to the drop-off area. "No one allowed in the pit" reads the sign, and I do obey. Have you taken a good look at the front-end loaders that beep and grind as they sweep away junk in the pit? Two loaders could play catch with my Prius.

Speaking of my car, I was embarrassed when backing into a slot by the wall. Surrounding me were Ford F-150s, Chevrolet Silverados, Honda 4 WD Pilots, and assorted trucks that apparently served in World War II. I tried not to compare vehicles, as I donned my work gloves and prepared to de-clutter both soul and garage. At least today I didn't have to pad my load with lame junk like a flat soccer ball circa 1998, cardboard boxes, a broken rake, and some moldy board I found in the backyard.

I had game this time. I had *serious* junk.

Not so fast, trash talker.

The guy next to me had hauled what looked like the remains of a small demolished city. I couldn't even identify his trash—was that a wall? A roof? A basement? A used Prius? To stall, I looked into the abyss that is my engine. Eventually, the man in the Ford F-150 finished his job, and somewhere in Maryland a county is missing a town.

I did not go into the pit. I did not stand on the wall. I did not scavenge.

I got to work.

And it was solitary and dirty and glorious work.

The jealous kind

September 15, 2013

Maybe you saw the item in "People in the News," which is one of my favorite newspaper features. I like reading about celebrity birthdays and romances especially when the news involves me.

Not by name, of course. I'm far too savvy about avoiding publicity—unlike *her.*

Do I sound bitter? I have every right to be. It's hard to pick up your hometown paper and see that your former lady friend is getting married. But that's exactly what Scarlett Johansson has done.

The actress is reportedly marrying a Frenchman and to add insult to fantasy, he's a former journalist. Granted, I'm a current journalist (last time I checked my pay check), but Scarlett is clearly drawn to us wordsmiths. I suppose this is her way of getting over me.

What Scarlett and I had was beyond words. Seriously, I have no words for it.

Oh, but she found a few.

"I don't like jealous behavior," she is quoted as saying. "It's really unattractive because it shows a sort of insecurity."

So now I'm insecure, too?

Why can't she just come out and say my jealousy and insecurity forced her into the arms of the Frenchman (no one, by the way, is ever forced into the arms of a Norwegian). My insecurity was that unattractive? Scarlett has conveniently forgotten how she used to think my insecurity was kind of cute.

Let me tell you how we met.

Several years ago, when I was a reporter for *The Baltimore Sun*, I interviewed Scarlett Johansson on the phone. She was staring in some Woody Allen movie.

Because this often happens between gorgeous celebrities and middle-aged, pouty features writer, we made a soul connection. Minutes on the phone with Scarlett felt like even more minutes. She made me laugh. I made her pretend to laugh. We didn't want the conversation to end even though her publicist on the other end of the phone broke in to tell me my 15 minutes were up.

We could have talked for 16 minutes—we had that much chemistry.

I'm not proud of how I acted next.

I became jealous when she married that Ryan Reynolds dude. I was jealous when she starred in movies with Owen Wilson, Javier Bardem, Matt Damon and God-knows-who-else in Hollywood.

She never said anything, but I know my jealousy put her off. After that 15-minute phone interview, we never spoke again. Nor did her publicist ever call me back.

The years have mellowed me. A nicked heart mends.

Would I have done anything differently?

Been less jealous, less insecure?

Yes, yes.

But I am the jealous kind.

Scarlett is marrying a man named Romain. Scarlett and Romain. Together, they will have gorgeous, leafy children. How can I compete with that?

No, I must move on and wish her all the happiness in the world with the Frenchman/former journalist whose arms I forced her into.

I won't stop loving because of Scarlett. I won't stop reading "People in the News," either.

Did you see where Raquel Welch turned 73?

73.

Still.

My resolutions (a.k.a. goals) for 2014

January 5, 2014

Change name to Carl, so when people ask if I'm related to the novelist Carl Hiaasen (he's my brother), I can say, "Why, no, kind but confused reader, I am the novelist. I'm merely moonlighting in Annapolis."

* * *

Change name back to Rob. Or Levi.

* * *

While walking dog in nearby cornfield, strive to keep him from eating deer hooves and other dead parts for no man should have to clean up the resulting Armageddon of intestinal events.

* * *

Dwell on more pleasant images in the new year.

* * *

Read five great books provided they are on the skinny side and don't keep me up past 10 on school nights.

* * *

Drink more or less or the same amount of red wine.

* * *

Keep options open re: wine.

* * *

Set goals. Goals are important. I know goals are important because I went to a meeting about goals, and I came away with the clear sense that goals are important. So, I'm going to set goals. You watch. I'll set so many goals your head will spin. In fact, your goal in 2014 will to stop me from setting so many goals.

* * *

Take time to remember wise words from beacons in my past, such as my high school guidance counselor who warned me: "Sarcasm is the lowest form of wit." She declined my request to forgo Algebra II. Goal denied.

* * *

Learn to spell Armageddon without having to look it up.

* * *

Plan now some sort of summer beach vacation and don't wait until July because by then the only rooms available are in my house.

* * *

Step foot in a church again to see if it still has that soulful old church smell.

* * *

Niagara Falls. Canadian side.

* * *

Re-assess my attraction to Mary Louise-Parker. With help from the psychiatric community, I hope to finally accept she is an actor and is not talking, making brown eyes at, or otherwise communicating only to me, Levi Hiaasen.

* * *

Gauge whether masquerading as a famous novelist will capture the heart of Mary Louise-Parker.

* * *

Seek additional therapy.

* * *

Visit my mom more—even if it means sleeping in the bed given me when I had not yet attained the height of four feet.

* * *

Solve the ancient mystery that is tipping.

* * *

Accept with grace, optimism and minimal pouting my 55th year.

* * *

Write. Breathe. Write. Breathe. Write.

* * *

Try to remember what the hell I ever did for fun.

* * *

Then have fun.

The Short List: In praise of pleasure

November 8, 2015

What pleasures make your short list?

In praise of...

Driving across the Bay Bridge (west-to-east) for no reason while listening to Paul Simon's "Graceland" very loudly.

In praise of...

Forgetting to eat at Chipotle for two years then remembering to eat at Chipotle and it was glorious.

In praise of...

Sleeping through the night.

In praise of...

Leaving ridiculously juvenile phone messages for my best friend since seventh grade who leaves ridiculously juvenile messages but mine are way better. I mean, what grown men impersonate key middle school teachers and pretend they are calling to ask us out on creepy dates 40 years later?

In praise of...

Hearing the wing-song from a formation of Canada Geese overhead.

In praise of...

Wood smoke.

In praise of...

Finding, against all odds in my dresser, matching socks—and a Macanudo Portofino cigar I bought 13 years ago and am still looking for an occasion to smoke down.

In praise of...

All check engine lights everywhere permanently dismantled by a loving, supreme being.

In praise of...

Not checking Twitter and Facebook for one whole day—or week—a mutiny!

In praise of...

John Irving writing a new novel.

In praise of...

My dog Earle finding a Twizzler escapee in the leaves outside the house the day after Halloween and devouring the Twizzler much like a Grizzly eviscerates a salmon.

In praise of...

Cheap, evaporating, globetrotting snow globes.

In praise of...

Thursdays. They are the week's month of May.

In praise of...

"You don't need a weatherman to know which way the wind blows"—Dylan.

In praise of...

Unexpected kindness. My mother's home health aide, en route yet again with her to dialysis, singing to her—with her—a song from long ago.

In praise of...

Good news from your children.

In praise of...

Driving across the Bay Bridge (east-to-west) for no reason while listening to Wilson Pickett's "Mustang Sally" very loudly. Check engine light be damned.

Taking a strange, unexpected and personal walk through our newspaper

April 22, 2017

The future looks to involve "24-hour leak-free security" and maybe a little sleepwalking

I was reading my newspaper the other day when an ad headline shook me to my core. My future passed before my eyes and points lower. Whatever self-doubts and setbacks that have dogged me were erased by this:

NEW ALTERNATIVE TO ADULT DIAPERS AND CATHETERS SETS MEN FREE.

Generally, I shy away from all caps (and New Year's Eve parties and poodles), but the news was so bold it deserved bold typography. Rather than having to wear diapers or use catheters, men can now use a skin-friendly pouch that "attaches to the tip of a man's anatomy." This, as my mother would say, is not dinner table talk. But by gosh, we need to talk about things that can set us free.

Believe me, I don't need "24-hour leak-free security." I'm not a long-haul truck driver who may or may not need an equivalent method for long-haul relief. I do have a longish commute to work, and I do like my morning coffee, but pouches have not entered into the equation. To recap: I don't need urological care of this or any magnitude, thank you very much. Psychiatry, sure, who doesn't? But not this really personal stuff.

Still.

How can you read such a thing and not see yourself down some long-haul, lonesome road from now?

Perhaps this cheery outlook explains a certain shortage of New Year's Eve parties.

* * *

I was reading my newspaper the other day and saw an item about a missing 98-year-old man. Fortunately, the man was found unharmed and was returned to his relieved family. Police reported the man does not have any medical issues, but he sleepwalks from time to time.

No medical issues at 98.

98.

Just sleepwalks away from home sometimes.

I am profoundly jealous of every fact in this story. Setting aside for the moment the worry such a missing invokes, I daydream of the day when I am 98 with no medical issues and slip away in sleep state and am returned unharmed to my loved ones.

Oh, he just walks off sometimes, they will tell police. Better check the water. He tends to wander down to City Dock to look at the water and boats.

And there they will find me. Sleepwalking and daydreaming among all the boats in all the water.

Found smiling, they will report.

* * *

I was reading my newspaper the other day about the FBI adding to its Ten Most Wanted Fugitives list the man suspected of killing his wife at a Dunkin' Donuts in Hanover two years ago. Police hope the renewed attention will produce fresh leads in the cold case.

The crime video is also back in the news with renewed views— many views. In the store video, the husband and wife are seen walking off-camera to a backroom and the husband emerging alone. For now it's the last image we have of the fugitive; it's forever the last image we have of his wife.

I watched the video as if vainly looking for clues. But what I was really watching was simply a woman walking with her husband to the backroom of where they worked. But she never comes back into camera range, no matter how many times I see the popular video. The story never changes.

For the people who knew and loved her, surely they must know countless strangers, such as myself, re-watched the last images of 21-year-old Palek Patel. If they could ask us why we watch, what would we say?

Oh, what a beautiful morning

March 8, 2015

Do you prefer sunrises over sunsets?

Are you a morning person?

(Good-bye.)

Do you love witnessing the break of dawn and never feel more alive than in the first glorious hours of the day?

(What's wrong with you?)

Do you prefer sunrises over sunsets?

(Check out my sunset pic.)

Do you break out in popular song first thing in the morning as you whip up French toast with strawberries and freshly-ground coffee?

(Please stop singing.)

Do you start your day with soul-stretching yoga, transcendental meditation, walking meditation or a spiritual meditation of your private making?

(Try the snooze button if you really want to rock your soul.)

Do you view each morning as an opportunity to express yourself through art, dance or acting in a one-act play you wrote in college and hope to one day have produced off-off-Broadway?

(Think matinee—at the earliest.)

Do you find that the sounds of morning epitomize beauty?

(Even the musical stylings of Yoko Ono?)

When you wake up with the chickens—and this still happens in some backyards—do you suddenly feel the urge to garden?

(Or feed the chickens?)

Do you consider each morning a brave, new opportunity to share the highlights of your last 10 years with your loved or liked one?

(No doubt windsurfing in Maui *was* swell.)

Do you read the newspaper first thing in the morning?

(Highly recommended. Hint, hint.)

Are you uncontrollably, certifiably happy in the morning?

(Good-bye.)

Does each morning present you the challenge of converting an unhappy morning person to a happy morning person?

(Sans a silo of mimosas.)

Does each morning present you with an unhappy morning person resisting such conversion?

(Need silo of mimosas.)

Do you hold animated, extended conversations if driving with someone first thing in the morning?

(Have you even been driven over a cliff?)

Do you feel the urge to strike out at the break of holy dawn to 1. fish. 2. hunt. 3. shop. 4. hike a substantial mountain. 5. enjoy a multigrain bagel at an outside table of a neighborhood eatery that knows you by name and life story?

(6. None of the above.)

Do you accomplish more in two morning hours than most people do in eight normal-human-being hours?

(Show-off.)

Do you find people who are not morning people prone to star-gazing, moon-howling, bathrobe wearing and TV viewing of Lifetime movies?

(Hey, don't knock "Deadly Honeymoon" or "Seduced by Lies." That's real life, missie.)

Do you ask yourself why bother with the rest of the day? Have you ever read Billy Collins' poem "Morning"?

(No, how does it go?)

Why do we bother with the rest of the day,
the swale of the afternoon,
the sudden dip into evening,
then night with his notorious perfumes,
his many-pointed stars?

This is the best —
throwing off the light covers,
feet on the cold floor,
and buzzing around the house on espresso —)
Are you converted?
(Not yet.)
Care for a mimosa?

Little did I know

February 10, 2018

What were you doing in 1959?

Me, not much.

But everyone else that year seemed to have been rockin' it. Take Rod Serling, that chain-smoking, supernatural storyteller who launched "The Twilight Zone" that year. If only he was still around to see "Black Mirror"—his mind-blowing, Netflix offspring. But who's to say Rod's spirit isn't planet-puddle-jumping through the universe?

NASA's Pioneer 4 spacecraft became the first American spacecraft to exit earth's orbit in 1959. Exciting stuff, for sure, but one Beechcraft Bonanza could have used NASA's ingenuity—or much better weather.

On the way to Fargo, North Dakota, the airplane went down in a cornfield and gone were "The Big Bopper," Ritchie Valens and Buddy Holly. The immortalized "Day the Music Died" was also the year of the first Grammy Awards. Justin Timberlake's performance and attire were also panned but excused on account of he hadn't been born.

The Baltimore Colts beat the New York Giants in the 1959 NFL championship. Winning players' share was $4,674—or the price of one of Tom Brady's shoelaces.

1959 was an entertaining year: on Broadway, "A Raisin in the Sun" debuted; on TV, "Bonanza" and "Rawhide" also debuted; at the movies, everyone either went to see Disney's "Sleeping Beauty" or "Ben-Hur," or both.

Me, I missed it.

Including news of Alaska and Hawaii joining the Union (*that's* why the TV show was called "Hawaii Five-0"). Fidel Castro took over Cuba, and thank you very much Mr. Castro and Mr. Nikita Khrushchev for that nuclear-charged, duck-and-cover drill launched a few years later.

Since there's no artful segue between these 1959 facts, here goes. Mattel's Barbie doll was introduced in pretty plastic. The Clutter family in Kansas was murdered in cold blood. History's bedfellows are seldom gift wrapped.

Oh, the best album was released. Don't attempt to argue with me. Just nod and accept and acknowledge my fortified opinion.

Miles Davis' "Kind of Blue." Next paragraph.

Mike Pence, "Weird Al" Yankovic and Jason Alexander of "Seinfeld" fame were born in 1959. Quick—what do they all have in common? I have no idea, but it might make a fun drinking game.

Speaking of something we all agree on, scientists were speaking about climate change in 1959. An excerpt from an article in the *Scientific American* in the same year:

"The theories that explain worldwide climate change are almost as varied as the weather ... Only the so-called carbon dioxide theory takes account of the possibility that human activities may have some effect on climate. This theory suggests that in the present century man is unwittingly raising the temperature of the earth by his industrial and agricultural activities."

And from the last paragraph:

"We shall be able to test the carbon dioxide theory against other theories of climatic change quite conclusively during the next half-century."

Fascinating stuff, but I missed it.

Because 59 years ago to this day in 1959, I was brought home from Fort Lauderdale's hospital. I imagine I spent my first day at home like I spend my Saturdays ever since—lounging, eating, staring, pondering.

Little did I know. Little do I know.

[10]
Man's Second
Best Friend

Good-bye my lovely

March 27, 2016

Capital columnist Rob Hiaasen sells off a family member for $100

We had to put the old girl down the other day.

It's hard losing a family member—even though she cost us a lot of money and heartache for nearly 20 years. She was part of our family, a running narrative onto herself.

But I had to make the call.

To one of the countless companies that offer money for your junk car.

Junk! How dare my 1997 Volvo 850 Sedan be called junk! How dare company X offer me $70, then another $50, then another $0 to tow my baby away. Each joint asks the same degrading questions. Each joint rips the heart out of you—as if cars can depreciate in our souls! As if you can put a dollar figure on family vacations, taking the kids to basketball or soccer practice, piano lessons, art lessons, and those endless orthodontist appointments.

Or all the other times it was just the kids in the car—tooling around town, listening to music loudly (my son, the first driver among my children, went through a Led Zeppelin-listening stage in the car, my daughters reported.) Or the time my oldest daughter ran over a curb at a Wendi's and popped the tire. Across the street was a fire station, where firefighters answered the call of flat tire duty. One was very cute, as reported to me.

Or the times I brought our dogs home to us, and the times I brought them to the vet for the last time.

And the time last week when I called around searching for a taker.

I called company Y, and the conversation went like this:

How many miles does the car have?

"Hard to say," I told the woman, who spoke from somewhere beneath the earth's crust.

My Volvo's odometer stopped ticking when the millennium was new.

"More than 300,000 but less than 500,000 miles?"

My generous parameters were greeted with radio silence.

"I really don't know how many miles the car has," I said, in limp concession.

Do you have a clear title?

Clear?

"Sure," I said. "It's clear. Very clear."

This seemed to satisfy company Y despite the fact I had no idea what I was talking about.

Does the car run?

By "run," did they mean can it still go forward or in reverse when asked? Technically, yes. I have seen my Volvo move. Not recently, but I have known it to move.

"Yes, it runs. Clearly."

I threw in "clearly" to impress them. Surely, company Y would now give me at least $1,000 for my baby, right? Maybe $1,500 for this darling fix-her-up!

Are there any missing parts on the car? Is there any damage to the vehicle?

Between you and me (and not company Y), the Volvo is a one-man show of accidents and mishaps:

- Side mirror sheered off by tree when car was driven one morning by someone who may or may not be my son. Do-it-yourself Duct tape job on mirror proves Duct tape doesn't *always* work.
- Ample chunk of back bumper went missing after car was parked on a busy street and got rammed and someone who may or may not have been my daughter was driving.
- Passenger side door crunched when the Volvo was parked at a Target. Again, a parent had not been driving the car.

- Muffler hasn't been seen in months, maybe years. You can hear the Volvo coming as if from Sweden.
- Felt material overhead became unglued and rests on head of driver like a soft veil. Downside: drooping roof lining obstructs one's view of road.
- A working AC? Please. That's like asking if the car can fly.
- Trunk lost its hydraulic abilities and comes down like a guillotine.
- Radio? CD player? What are these listening devices you speak of?
- The horn works. I know because I replaced it once.

"The car is missing a small piece of bumper and has a dent in the side," I said.

$100, they said.

They will give me $100 for the clear title and car and then clearly tow it away. Best offer.

OK, I said.

What more can you say or do after 20 years?

Rest in peace, car.

We had a time, didn't we?

Man's second best friend

September 8, 2013

You know the feeling.

I don't mean to bring anyone down—not with the Market House opening (it *is* open, right?)—but I have one of those lousy decisions to make.

She's been with me for almost 14 years. She has been such a loyal girl, so full of pep in her day, so pretty.

The girl has gone about everywhere with me. We had adventures together. We vacationed together. Rain or shine, she was by my side.

Then age caught up with her, and it's become too expensive to keep her alive. I hate feeling that way, but I can't afford to keep her going.

It's time to say goodbye.

But, damn, she's been a good car.

I remember the day we brought my 1997 Volvo 850 home—her shiny maroon coat, her soft plush seats, her multiple CD player. When I took her out, she ran smooth, fast and true.

I always felt safe with her.

For 10 years, she was rock solid. Then, the inevitable slide.

It was the little things at first.

Her seat warmer stopped warming. Yes, there are far greater problems in the world, but I couldn't think of any worse than those winter nights in my chilly-seated Volvo.

Her multiple CD player, without a courtesy warning, stopped multiplying.

Her odometer stopped working somewhere in the first Bush administration. Who knows, the car might now have 600,000 miles on her.

Her check engine light began to taunt me like a tell-tale heart.

And what they call those turn signal and windshield wiper things stopped working. And the trunk didn't want to close. And a funky mildew smell took up permanent residence.

Oh, and my kids learned to drive.

Suddenly, murky traffic-related events occurred, the facts of which remain elusive to this day. My Volvo took a beating in parking lots, on multiple Beltways, in friends' driveways. Literal chunks of the car went missing. I would hear her weep at night.

And, always, the relentless beating of the check engine light...

The bills piled up and somehow always rounded off to $500. Those are what I call the good old days. Then came bills rounded off to $1,000. I diligently speared all my car's expenses to a nail over my work bench until one night I burned them all.

That night I realized our relationship was strained beyond repair.

The last few months have been downright ugly.

My Volvo sounds like an air boat. If you ever had the pleasure of a scenic air boat ride, you know it culminates in a renewed appreciation for nature and temporary hearing loss. I'm hoping a muffler is still attached to my Volvo, but I'm afraid to look.

Last month, my car failed its emissions test. Of course. Who was she trying to fool? I took the car to my mechanic, who said the repair would cost $1,000. Of course.

Nevermore.

It's over.

Through no fault of her own, my Volvo grew old and cranky and unreliable. I can't blame her. I thank her.

She was my girl, who now looks up as if to say, please. Do it now. Please.

Let me go.

My own bridge scandal

January 19, 2014

I stand before you today, not so much standing for it is Sunday morning and I have not yet left my bed, but the point is I need to apologize to the people of Maryland.

Many of you experienced the unsanctioned closing of four of the Chesapeake Bay Bridge's five lanes this month. The closings, which were not authorized by me, created a traffic jam the likes of which William Preston Lane Jr. himself could never have imagined. For those too young to remember, William Preston Lane Jr., the Bay Bridge's namesake, was a former Maryland governor. I think he also played for the Buffalo Bills in the old AFL.

The Bay Bridge is a vital, mirroring link connecting two great shores and two great peoples: the people who can't wait to get to the other side, and the people who can't wait to get to the *other* side, and please stop honking I'm moving as fast as I can. Both great peoples pass like cranky ships in the day and night on the bridge, as it should be and has been.

It was John Smith who, when first stepping foot on our pristine shores, proclaimed, "Sure, the oyster population is hopping, but how will future generations cross this great water to get to Ocean City without a modest, open, wooden ship such as my own?"

Springing from those noble words centuries later came the construction of the first span of the Bay Bridge. The span, then called William Preston, opened in 1952. The second, completing span opened in 1973 and was fully named William Preston Lane Jr.

Given this storied background, it is with additional remorse that I publicly assume responsibility for what I discovered was an intentional and politically-motivated lane closure.

When the story broke I told the media the lane closings were part of a traffic study, and that no one in my administration recommended or participated in any such action for petty or political motives. Despite my signature honesty, the story would not go away because, as I have painfully learned, the press would rather question me than adore me.

Consider this partial transcript of my Jan. 2 press conference held at Sandy Point State Park following the incident:

Reporter: "Mr. Hiaasen, you publicly stated the lane closings were part of a traffic study. What traffic study?"

Me: "While I have always respected the constitutional role of journalism in our free society, I will not answer personal attacks on my character."

Reporter: "I was just asking what traffic study you were conducting that warranted the random closing of four lanes during rush hour Friday afternoon."

Me: "How would you like it if I ambushed *you* at a state park and asked what traffic study *you* are working on?"

Reporter: "But I never said I was working on a traffic study, and you invited reporters here."

Me: "That's exactly my point."

The story still didn't die. So, this past week I held personal discussions with my senior staff. I also asked to review their emails, Instagram and Tumblr. accounts, high school report cards and childhood diaries. These investigative measures were not related to the lane closings, but I enjoyed them just the same.

It's clear now I was deceived regarding the Jan. 2 lane closures. It should be equally clear that I'm in charge and take full responsibility. My senior staff members have all been terminated. And while homicide is a serious offense, I take more seriously my commitment to the people of Maryland.

Later today, I pledge to stand in the middle of the Chesapeake Bay Bridge and personally stop and apologize to every commuter.

I also pledge to first grab a shower and get dressed.

Unmentionable driving crimes

October 20, 2013

There's been a lot of talk about the danger of texting while driving. Talking on your cellphone is also a dangerous idea and illegal. But Maryland lawmakers have not gone far enough to criminalize other driving behaviors.

What makes me qualified to advise Maryland on additional regulations?

My life on the road.

Every day my commute takes me on a miasma of interstates and beltways and through tunnels with lousy radio reception.

My round trip affords me ample time to observe the driving habits of my brethren with time left to finish my novel, double check the meaning of "miasma" and dissect every turning point in my life that led me to this commute.

But here's the difference between me and *them:* While I use my commute creatively and philosophically, other drivers are breaking the law. Not yet, mind you, but they will be breaking the law if I have my way with the General Assembly.

Beginning January 2014, I propose all drivers stuck in traffic and heard singing the following will be subject to fine and/or imprisonment:

- Any Katy Perry single.
- "Sweet Home Alabama."
- "Don't Stop Believing."
- "Love Shack."
- Any show tune.

First-time offenders would be fined $50. Drivers incurring a second offense would lose their licenses for 30 days. A third offense would land motorists in any of our federal penitentiaries, where singing restrictions also apply.

Reckless singing, however, pales in comparison to other disturbing behaviors. We've all heard of "Road Rage," but I've become more concerned with "Road Relief." I suspect there are laws already on the books involving this behavior, but lawmakers need to strengthen those laws.

Perhaps you, too, have witnessed the scene:

Commuters are gridlocked due to a fender bender clearly off the road and not impacting traffic, yet traffic has come to a standstill in compulsive observance of said minor fender bender. Nearby, one driver has parked on the shoulder and exited his car.

Look at him standing there, enjoying the idyllic vista only an interstate can offer—trees, bushes, graffiti, roadkill. Look at how he has left the passenger door open and is standing behind it like a nervous statue.

Look no more, fellow travelers.

The driver is relieving himself.

As a fellow guy, I am not without sympathy. Nature has us on speed dial sometimes. But on a Friday afternoon when my commuting time magically doubles, I just want to get home. I'm not in the mood for Katy Perry or that dude over there hiding behind his car door.

I'm sensible enough to know we can't legislate all human behavior. I'm sensible enough not to call for severe prison sentences for people who change lanes in tunnels or give my Prius dirty liberal looks.

But "Don't Stop Believing" and roadside relieving?

Can't they wait until they get home?

'Love Shack' Redux

November 10, 2013

In a writing career spanning more than three decades and earning me literally thousands of dollars, I've made my share of typos, misspellings, and gaffes. But I've never apologized for anything I've written.

Except one time.

Many years ago, in a feature on a sick woman, I meant to write how "everyone loves her sense of humor." Instead the sentence appeared as "everyone loves her sense of tumor." Since tumors are rarely funny, I felt it necessary to apologize. To the whole family. Repeatedly.

Now, I find myself in the awkward position of having to apologize again.

I wrote a column in this space Oct. 20 that chronicled my frustrations when driving my long commute. Among the "unmentionable driving crimes" were people caught singing while we're stuck in traffic. I recommended federal prison terms for repeat offenders.

I still stand by my recommendation, but I feel compelled to apologize for citing one song. Four readers gently scolded me for including the B-52's "Love Shack" on my list of banned songs—along with tunes, "Don't Stop Believing," "Sweet Home Alabama," and any Katy Perry song. No objections there.

Because I respect my single-digit readership, I felt it was my journalistic—no, humane—obligation to reconsider the merits of "Love Shack." I haven't heard the song in awhile, so I tracked it down employing modern techniques culminating in asking a friend to pretty please find the song for me.

With new, open ears, I listened again to . . .

The love shack is a little old place where we can get together
Love Shack, baby (a-Love Shack, baby)
Love Shack, baby, Love Shack

Love Shack, baby, Love Shack

Love Shack, baby, Love Shack (Love, baby, that's where it's at)

Love Shack, baby, Love Shack (Love, baby, that's where it's at)

And because I remembered all the words (who doesn't?) I sang along again to . . .

Huggin' and a-kissin'

Dancin' and a-lovin'

Wearin' next to nothin'

'Cause it's hot as an oven

The whole shack shimmies

Yeah, the whole shack shimmies

Remember the video? Of course, you do. *Rolling Stone* voted "Love Shack" the best single of 1989. And in a saucy tribute, adult video stores named their businesses after the song. How could I publicly call for the jailing of people singing . . .

Hop in my Chrysler, it's as big as a whale and it's about to set sail

I got me a car, like, it seats about 20

So come on and bring your jukebox money

How could I?

Bang, bang, bang, on the door, baby

Knock a little louder, baby

Bang, bang, bang, on the door, baby

I can't hear you

I hear you my dear four readers. I was wrong about "Love Shack." It's a fun, great song. Let me hear you sing it on I-97 Friday afternoons. Hell, I'll sing it with you.

Your what?

Tin roof, rusted

Exactly.

The mother of all nature

February 16, 2014

I'm not wired for snow.

I was born on the scorching, barren outskirts of the Florida Everglades. I didn't see snow until I was 23, and even then I saw it from inside my Toyota Corolla and didn't leave my car because it was snowing.

Yes, snow can be scenic and alluring. So can Angelina Jolie, but she can be *scary*, too.

(It's difficult transitioning from Angelina Jolie to my inept snow driving, so I'll skip any attempt at an artful transition.)

I'm not wired to drive in the snow.

There are many safe and sensible ways to drive in wintry conditions. Few come to my mind. So, I will share a Floridian's tips and observations for driving in inclement weather:

1. First, let's not say "inclement." It's a weird word. Let's say the weather is lousy or something like that.

2. Judging by commuters this past week, the general rule when driving in the snow is go either 25 miles under the speed limit or 25 miles over it. I recommend going a reasonable speed under the speed limit, but I appear to be alone on this.

3. Despite one's inclination to notice the intriguing profile of the motorist crawling along side you on I-97, keep your eyes on the road at all times. I don't follow this recommendation, but let's not spoil the spirit of this tip.

4. I have learned ice is worse than snow; meaning: it's safer to drive in an angelic, Robert Frost-like snowfall than it is to lose control of your car on ice and go careening off-road toward Certain and Final Death.

5. Doesn't "black ice" sound like a teenage boy's deodorant? A new bourbon? Sure it does—until it causes Certain and Final Death.

6. When leaving your car outside before a snow, lift up your windshield wipers. I'm not sure what this does, but it's fun driving around with those things poking up.

7. When following behind salt trucks, increase your braking distance to 3.5 miles. We didn't have salt trucks in Florida; we had festive, seasonal carjackings.

8. When driving in the snow and your visibility is reduced to "God Help Me I Can't See My Dashboard," pull safely off the road *under an overpass*. Never pull safely off the road *over an underpass*. It's snowing up there, I learned.

9. Finally, if you find yourself skidding, follow these steps:

A. Don't panic (short bursts of primal screaming are acceptable).

B. Take your foot off the gas pedal.

C. Take your frightened hand off your passenger's equally frightened thigh.

D. Don't hit the brakes.

E. Steer in the direction of the skid. If you don't know what direction you are skidding in, call to mind a prayer you might have memorized in childhood.

Finally, probably the most important tip:

10. If you loathe winter to the very marrow of your sunny soul, do what I do. Turn privately against co-workers, family, friends, strangers, drivers, cats, housewives from New Jersey, cats from New Jersey, and people from your past who declined to attend a high school homecoming dance with you even though they promised they would.

Thank you and safe driving.

My brush with the law & other fun stories

February 21, 2016

Far be it for me to utter an editorial syllable on any local matter of news. That's not my job. That job requires a lot of thinking, and my thinker tends to get sore and cranky.

But I do believe I have a solution to this recurring school board nominating drama.

To artfully recap, some want an elected 9-member board; some want an appointed board like we have now; and others want a hybrid of appointed and elected. Others want racial diversity on the board, an old-fashioned concept apparently out of fashion.

Still others want board members to be appointed only in leap years (this year, for example) provided the moon is in the seventh house and Jupiter aligns with Mars. Others want a 25-member board consisting only of student representatives between the ages of 6 through 9. Critics have decried the school board for skewing older and being "out of touch with the kids." School board meetings would have two nap periods, one snack time, and everyone home by dinner.

All quality ideas, but there's something better.

Mired in traffic on I-97, I had time to reflect on the issue (and on the fact my CD player and Sirius don't work and why others don't seem alarmed). I've never served on a school board or any board—although I had a neighbor once who would have been a fine school board member because she was so involved and caring about everything-schools that I could barely stand to listen to her after 15 minutes.

I'm not a fan of boards or meetings or really any group of people meeting to discuss anything. One person should be the school board. That person would make all the decisions, and everyone would have to obey.

Just elect a great Mom.

She'll take care of the rest.

* * *

Don't know if this gives us a sense of spring, but it's got a sense of humor.

At Knightongale Farms in Davidsonville on Solomons Island Road, there's a spidey round bale of hay with a lot of heart.

Finally, a romantic use for flexible drain pipes.

* * *

Speaking of free fun, I lost some.

There's a side street by the office here that leads to a green water pond. In this fenced pond are turtles—two, sometimes three moss-backed turtles emerge to float in suspended animation. I don't catch them. I don't hurt them. I just watch for them. My free fun.

There I was turtle watching late last year when a law officer approached. Perhaps I looked suspicious in my work clothes standing there in suspended animation. I had thrown a rock in the pond to see how far I could still throw. More free fun—and further evidence my throwing ain't what it used to be.

"I give up," the officer said. "What are you doing?"

I told him about the turtles. He said I was trespassing and needed to leave.

For a split second, I felt like a turtle-watching outlaw! A trespasser!!

Then I felt lousy and left.

There shouldn't be anything wrong with watching for turtles.

So, Anne Arundel doesn't welcome us?

April 20, 2016

It's the little things.

I've never committed to that phrase because clearly it's often the really big things. But "it's the little things" comes in handy when managing reader expectations on the eve of a little story.

Say you commute to work from Anne Arundel to Prince George's County and Bowie or beyond. Say you drive Route 50 every week day across those county lines. Surely, you have noticed the perky blue road sign welcoming you across the border: "Welcome to Prince George's County. On the Path to Greatness." On the path to greatness indeed! Or perhaps just simply on a path to your job.

Say you drive home the same way when lo and behold, as you cross the Patuxent River, you look up to see the grand, brick-layered, night-lit sign welcoming you back to Anne Arundel County, where every path is great!

Only the sign doesn't say anything these days. No welcoming words, no arms-coated county seal, nothing but blank brick sunning itself au naturel.

Then you notice the world still spinning because this is a very little thing.

Still.

What's up with the missing sign?

And what's up with the blank road sign just west of it?

I smell a blank sign conspiracy—person or persons systematically with snail-like timing erasing the signage of Anne Arundel County. If left to their civic tricks, the culprits will soon reduce our roadways to nothing but trees and streams and farm land! Commuters won't know where the hell they are! Only that Prince George's County will be left standing in all its pretty blue signage!

I'm not going to stand for this.

I'm going to sit and make a few calls.

The inherent danger of gathering information is you run the risk of discovering facts that flay and gut your conspiracy theories, which, if you don't golf or fish or whatever, aren't the worst hobbies.

First, as for the second sign on Route 50, it's one of those national Sponsor-A-Highway deals. The sponsor, Royal Farms, left the program April 1, so down came the road sign plug for the grocery chain. Another sponsor is being lined up, we're told by the sponsor highway folks in California. They didn't appear alarmed by this routine change of sign business, so we calmed down.

But then we contacted Anne Arundel County officials about the missing welcoming sign. We demanded answers, politely, in an email. Surely, private investigators if not the FBI are on the case.

Not so much.

Launched by former County Executive Janet Owens, five such signs greet motorists at points of the county's compass, and they all have been neutered of lettering. Our county gateways are blank slabs of nothingness.

Well, crews are re-working the signs, the first maintenance in a decade. Removing and adding new letters, re-pointing and sealing the brick, and acid washing will cost about $5,900 a sign.

By the end of the month, "Welcome to Anne Arundel County" should grace all 5 signs once again.

There is no conspiracy. No FBI involvement. It's not even a low-grade mystery.

It's just a column lost on the path to greatness.

When the cobra strikes

March 30, 2014

"In its palmy days the Model T could take off faster than anything on the road."

- From E.B. White's "Farewell, My Lovely!"

Today, E.B. White would be 114 years and 261 days old. In celebration of this milestone, I dusted off a collection of his essays. When I'm in need of religion, I return to the altar of my favorite White pieces, "Once More to the Lake," "On a Florida Key" and "Afternoon of an American Boy."

Then something happens, and I discover an essay I had overlooked. "Farewell, My Lovely!" was White's torch song to the revolutionary, indomitable Model T Ford. "It was," White wrote in 1936, "the miracle God has wrought."

"The driver of the old Model T was a man enthroned."

"Springtime in the heydey of the Model T was a delirious season. Owning a car was still a major excitement."

"The days were golden, the nights were dim and strange."

Well, read the essay if for no other reason than to stop me from quoting Mr. White.

I'm too young to have been enthroned on a Model T. I was enthroned on a green 1971 Corolla that got me where I wanted to go and then some. My Corolla never inspired delirium or an essay, but you should have seen my gold shag carpet and happening 8-track. I've been a Toyota man ever since. But I learned to drive on a '66 Ford Mustang, and years later the urge to own a new Mustang has invaded my soul with the swarming determination of cicadas.

Last week I found myself tip-toeing onto a Ford dealership hoping not to be approached by humans selling cars. There, in a back row, a charcoal black Mustang with a V6 Pony Package winked at me. I don't know what a VC Pony Package entails except it was one cool car. The kind of car that looks so fast you could get a speeding ticket for standing by it. The kind of car that looks a mid-life crisis right in the eyes and says, "This ain't no crisis. This is a rebirth!"

The kind of car that in its palmy days can go from zero to 60 in 3.5 seconds.

I read that stat in my glossy Mustang brochure. (Can one marry a brochure? Legally probably not, but maybe some kind of civil ceremony?) The brochure alone can make a sensible man give up his sensible Prius. Leave the bug humming on the side of I-97.

Consider the Shelby GT500 Mustang.

"Its rumble. Unmistakable. This cobra's ready to strike."

Or the GT.

"Any way you spec it—a visceral thrill ride."

Or the V6.

"With plenty of low-end grunt and twin independent variable camshaft timing."

Low-end grunt? Is that how you tell when your Mustang is cranky or really happy? Clearly, there's so much I don't know about the Mustang.

Yet, I want one. I want it to be very fast—like a visceral, low-end grunting cobra. And I'll drive this cobra every day until that one strange day when I pass all my usual exits and keep going on some open, lonesome, thrilling road, just like in the brochure.

Farewell, my lovelies.

[11]
From Flights of Fancy

In a sentence, Donald Trump is a bluffer (or How I spent my Summer Vacation)

August 9, 2015

How I spent my vacation with Donald Trump

So, I was in Ireland at McDermott's pub in Doolin when I got talking to two older Irish gentlemen whose English resembled my Gaelic, which is to say we weren't following each other when —

the gentleman with the Irish-character-actor hair and mug, after recommending a whiskey that started with P or K, looked up from his stout and through his forest-thick eyebrows presented me with a statement concerning —

politics, a subject I zealously avoid, but I was weary from driving on the other side of the road dodging shrubs, sheep, goats, and motor coaches, so I had another stout and wanted to listen to anything to take my mind off dying-while-vacationing when the man said —

Donald Trump is a bluffer! —

which were about the only words I understood in each other's company for an hour on account I had stumbled into a —

wake, an Irish wake for an innkeeper and not just any innkeeper but the man who ran the storied lodge I was staying in and who had passed away the day before my arrival which was sadder that it should have been since I never met the man and it raised the question of—

whether the lodge would even be open given this man was beloved and important and yes, the restaurant and bar closed from shock alone, but the room was still available which was bittersweet but convenient since I had driven cross-country from Dublin on the other side of the road and it's true—what they say about Irish wakes, they are uplifting, and when I remarked about the man's passing an Irish woman said, God took him, so I ordered a whiskey that started with P or K and asked the Donald Trump man if —

he had heard of Martin O' Malley, no, he said, Hillary Clinton, and that name didn't seem to register either but Donald Trump is a bluffer, a new word on me and you know when you discover a new word you just can't —

stop using it, so I'm still going around saying the word bluffer, bluffer, bluffer, because learning new words in new places is the best along with —

learning anything in a new place about the people, the land, yourself, Irish wakes, Irish writers, sheep, toy rental cars, the mystery that are European adapters, seafood chowder X, seafood chowder Y, seafood chowder Z, a fish called turbot, a setter named Nellie, and this about bagpipes —

Scottish bagpipes are mouth-driven; Irish bagpipes are armpit-driven and —

everywhere I saw stone hedgerows, planetarium skies, bi-polar weather, black-wrapped bales of hay with the occasional pink wrapping for breast cancer awareness, a novel rural demonstration I thought while trying to keep my eyes on the road and not count pink bales and —

miss yet another unmarked road that laughs at GPS, oh Irish local roads, you bluffers! —

two hands on the wheel —

two hands on the wheel —

and one night I met John and Mary from near Cork and met Steve and Melissa from Wyoming at one pub then days later at a castle because sometimes you run into the same people on vacation anywhere you go and it's a little awkward because the last time you saw them you all thought would really be the last time but then people sometimes —

reappear! like weird vacation magic and learning the lingo —

half nine instead of 9:30 and Cheers or Mind Yourself when saying goodbye and me losing track of the towns starting with K and —

Beckett's *Waiting for Godot* and Joyce's *Dubliners* and Wilde's *De Profundis* and the —

Cliffs of Moher —

Cliffs of Moher —

finally, my mother's maiden name in County Clare printed on trucks and restaurant signs and feeling fractionally home —

home by another way.

Once more to McDermott's Pub in Ireland

March 18, 2018

"The light music of whiskey falling into glasses made an agreeable interlude."—James Joyce

There are many unfair things—and this is one of them: For St. Patrick's Day, we should be able to resurrect a dead Irish writer for a day of agreeable interlude. Just one day before returning them to their roused earth to resume resting in peace.

Resting in peace? Ha! Imagine a Joycean response to that sentimental conviction! Life, as the Irish say, will break your heart. Death can't be an upgrade, can it?

See, I have questions.

Many so-called Irish bars are named after Joyce (including one in Baltimore). But for our day together, he and I should meet at McDermott's Pub in Doolin, County Clare. The bar is perfectly not fancy although the Irish beef stew came close to perfect. The Guinness was Guinness. Is it better in Ireland? Don't know or care.

But there is a cold, spidery creek running outside the pub's chunky property. If I were a smoker, I would smoke there. If I were a poet, I would poet there. But I was just a tourist who walked back into the pub for another pint.

"Every life is in many days, day after day. We walk through ourselves, meeting robbers, ghosts, giants, old men, young men, wives, widows, brothers-in-love, but always meeting ourselves."

Three summers ago I stumbled into the middle of a wake at McDermott's. Inside, darkly, there were young and old men, wives and widows and definitely ghosts and giants. We were all there to meet ourselves.

I also met a man, in full Irish wake mode, who was having a pint and talking American politics because there's only so much you can say about a dead man no matter his surviving charms.

"Donald Trump is a bluffer!" the man said. (Again, this was 2015.) I needed to be told what a bluffer was.

The Irish have a way with words—unlike that sentence.

"Think you're escaping and run into yourself. Longest way round is the shortest way home."

A toast to Joyce, the Wanderer King. I have this round, by the way.

Get this. Joyce had 19 addresses in 22 years during what has been described as his voluntary exile in Dublin. He was a man at devout work. He also had to keep leaving home to understand home.

How many addresses have the rest of us had?

I had five in five years and once, four in one year—badges of restlessness carried for no reason.

What good do all our addresses do? Where do they really lead us?

It's always about the shortest way home.

Another round?

"The sacred pint alone can unbind the tongue."

Benjamin Franklin—not Irish—said something about beer being proof God loves us or something along those lines.

Joyce's lines were better—although his novels don't make for breezy beach reading. I tried to read *Ulysses*. I ended up falling in love with his words and not his story.

But how wonderful it is to leave in your wake words that are more than enough for some.

Does everything magical have to be a story?

See, I have questions.

Rise then, Joyce.

Join me once more at McDermott's, and when it's very late we'll go outside by the creek and talk of ghosts and giants.

Portable Paris: An immoveable feast

August 13, 2017

If you are fortunate enough to be planning a trip to Paris, then you know the library of travel books and websites available to you. Fodor's. Frommer's. Rick Steves. The Little Black Book of Paris. Scores of others.

There's also Paris by word-of-mouth. Everyone who goes to Paris returns with 46.8 (on average) itinerary and culinary suggestions for friends and family to absorb and consider. This speaks, of course, to the fullness of Paris.

My advice—having just returned from France in one dreamier and fatter piece—is to experience Paris on your own terms. If you need to watch Woody Allen's "Midnight in Paris" or read Hemingway's "A Moveable Feast" to get in the mood, do it. While I can't compete with *Messieurs* Eugene Fodor and Arthur Frommer, I am qualified to offer my own tips for the Paris-bound adventurer.

About the churches. They are old, hallowed and free. Just walk right in. If the front door is locked or sealed, visitors are asked to enter the old, hallowed, free church by a side door. The tip: The side door looks like any normal, non-church door. The side door is *not* the towering, 200-year-old wooden door before you and that looks like it's been immoveable for 200 years. Do not try and open the door.

The majestic, ancient door will make a horrible scraping sound that will not only alert and offend church caretakers and visitors but will wake the saints. They will not be pleased, either. In the event of this *faux pas*, do not attempt to close the 200-year-old door you pried opened. Just drop what you're doing and flee France.

About the hotel bathrooms. They are small, not hallowed and costly. The bathtubs are unusually deep (and given the apparent trend, the shower half-doors guarantee a soaked bathroom floor). Americans, with their shallow tubs, aren't accustomed to rappelling out of a French bathtub. The tip: practice stepping in and out of your deep tub before showering. It's a long way down.

For if you are not practiced at the art of Parisian bathtub exiting, you might find yourself face-and-body down on the watery bathroom floor. You might have injured minor or major parts to your vacationing body. You might be indelicately splayed out, like a broken sculpture model, until help arrives. And while it might be an amusing story for later, the present shock and pain of the fall will momentarily threaten not only your Trip of a Lifetime but your will to leave your hotel room.

About the hotel pool. If you are really fortunate and your hotel has a pool, embrace it. Make friends with your hotel pool for chances are your French pool will be a water work of art, a placid becalming being. German and British and Australian and American and French people will encircle the *piscine*. The tip: the pool is for polite wading or maybe a few non-competitive breaststrokes. It is not a lap or play pool. One should not channel their innermost child and execute a cannonball.

For the cannonball could effect the young, fashionable French couple sitting next to you and who haven't said a word to you or even looked at you in your shark-patterned American swim trunks. You have splashed them on their microscopic threads of fabric that pass for swimming attire. You will not be sharing a bottle of *rosé* down along the hypnotic Seine with them any time soon or ever.

Messieurs Fodor and Frommer don't address these possibilities. They offer choice itineraries, safety tips, electrical adjustments, bistros vs. brasseries, gargoyles, tipping and how to order *vin rouge*. They offer primers on French social culture. Like staring at a total solar eclipse, it's advised not to look directly at French people. Sustained eye contact can be construed as rude or sexually-tinted. In turn, they won't be looking at you (except for your shoes). Don't take it personally.

The tip proved invaluable to a certain ego.

For not a single French woman at the pool stared at the snazzy shark swim trunks on the bruised American tourist who nearly broke a 200-year-old church door.

Tequila, Blue Angels and Iguanas

April 6, 2016

What do you get when you mix tequila, iguanas and Blue Angels? Vacation.

Can't a man get away?

I was sitting in a bar in Key West questioning another Hemingway myth while questioning the tequila volume in my margarita when the guy next to me mentions he's from Annapolis.

Had I heard about their yacht club fire a few months back?

Yes.

It was quite the fire, he said.

Yes, yes, it was.

I ordered another margarita in hopes of avoiding work-related chat and in profound hopes of acquiring more tequila.

Some time later (an hour? three?) I broke from the famous bar to re-introduce myself to sunlight. It's a very bright world in Key West when you're not in a bar. I hopped on my rental bike—with its unhip basket and sexy wobble—and repaired to one of the compact, imperfect beaches native to the Keys.

There, under a palm tree intelligently designed for relaxation, I heard the roar of jets. Others stopped to stare into the Windex blue sky. They were amazed at what they saw. They were speechless. They paused in mid-drink. I looked, but I knew what jets make those dramatic, darting sounds.

What are they? the beach people asked.

The Blue Angels, I said. (From the Naval base at Key West.)

Never before have I been so knowledgeable after so many margaritas.

* * *

You do miss local news when you're away.

Taylor Swift is moving to Annapolis!

Taylor Swift is NOT moving to Annapolis!

Oh.

It was just an April Fools' Day trick that went viral.

While perusing my vacation newspaper, *The Key West Citizen*, I looked for its own gag story on April 1—maybe something like Prohibition returning to the Keys. But no, the paper had its typical, run-of-South-Florida headlines:

"Tourists yelled at for saying hello"

"Woman wielding switchblades demands Prozac"

Just another day in paradise.

* * *

Later, I was sitting by the pool self-administering tequila into a margarita when I noticed a banded garden hose draped over the privacy fence. The Keys have such funky garden hoses. Funky everything, particularly its Prozac crowd.

Then the 18-inch garden hose slithered over the fence.

Soon, the rest of the iguana surfaced and perched atop of tin roof to announce with great stillness and command that the pool area belonged to him.

He was beautiful.

Or she.

The Keys are overrun by the invasive iguana, which is destroying gardens and invading cemetery crypts while eating fruit and critters normally not prey. Apparently, a market for iguana meat is developing although I skipped any taste test (iguana road kill is also prevalent—and messy—in the Keys these days). Everywhere I turned, paddled, swam, walked or biked, I saw iguanas in various stages of lurking, repose and friskiness.

One crawled along the tin roof as I slept one night. Judging by the sound and scratching, I thought it was a Velociraptor. But no, it was just my poolside iguana, Key West's new king of the jungle.

Finally, something that didn't remind me of Annapolis.

Finally, a getaway.

Hello, I'm not working today

August 7, 2016

How to have fun on vacation: don't over think, don't think

If you are reading this (first, thank you), then please know I'm on vacation.

I wrote this awhile back in anticipation of my time off. Why? Because my commitment to writing is unparalleled in American journalism. On a more nuanced note, I pre-wrote my vacation column in the wildest, gravest hope that I'm having fun—today—on my vacation.

Vacations are vexing. The pressure of getting away, the pressure of relaxing, the pressure of packing, the pressure of tipping, the pressure of not-thinking-about-work, the pressure of having *fun*. Reminds me of a poem Elizabeth Bishop wrote about her old friend, Robert Lowell. From Bishop's "North Haven":

Years ago, you told me it was here
(in 1932?) you first "discovered girls"
and learned to sail, and learned to kiss.
You had "such fun," you said, that classic summer.
("Fun"—it always seemed to leave you at a loss...)

The poem's last line never leaves me at a loss.

By now you are mighty glad you don't have to go on vacation with me. Nothing says summer fun more than a guy reciting downer poetry while dissecting the meaning of fun and realizing via work emails the newsroom merrily thrives in his absence.

But a man can change, right?

Here's my pre-vacation checklist in the hopes when summer break is over, my answers suggest a new and improved man:

Did you attempt to leave your La-Z-Boy? A. Yes. B. No. C. Maybe.

Did you attempt to leave your house? (Staring at the moss growing out of your age-old paved driveway does not count—nor does mail retrieval, suspiciously eyeing a UPS truck that dared to deliver something next door, or going outside to consider washing your car before changing your mind.) A. Yes. B. No. C. Don't understand the question.

Assuming you left your chair and home, describe your mood: A. Cheerfully receptive to grand adventures. B. Cautious yet willing to embrace unproven adventures. C. Subdued; catatonic. D. Visibly upset Elizabeth Bishop didn't write a poem about me.

Assuming you encountered fun, did you: A. Frolic in its fun, loving arms. B. Appreciate the fun—from a safe distance. C. Seek shelter in your La-Z-Boy. D. Ask to see fun's I.D.

Assuming you had a good vacation, would you: A. Be open to leaving your chair/house next summer. B. Bring your La-Z-Boy along with you on vacation. C. Not read your work emails or poetry. D. All of the above.

And now, having exhausted myself, I need to get back to not working.

Have you tried snow snorkeling?

March 21, 2018

They say it's spring.

That's the name of an old jazz song I heard for the first time this week. It's important to have firsts—especially when you are snowed in.

Consider magic, for example.

I don't believe in most magic, but I believe in the ability of inanimate objects to have real conversations. It also might help to know my Weber grills have long been my imaginary friends. They, too, were stuck in the storm called Toby.

Gas Grill: *"What kind of name is Toby for a storm? Why not Timmy—Winter Storm Timmy?"*

Kettle Grill: *"Are you serious?"*

GG: *"No, I'm cold. You?"*

KG: *"Been warmer."*

GG: *"I hear you."*

KG: *"I know a way we can warm up."*

GG: *"I like the way you think, Timmy."*

KG: *"Help me off with this coat, Toby. We got some grillin' to do."*

I don't know what they have planned. They asked me to leave on account we've had "incidents" involving my wielding of an over-sized grill spatula. A restraining order was floated out there, but I don't know its legal status.

What's clear is I need something to do besides listening to old jazz songs and dreaming of hamburgers, hot dogs, corn and Caesar salad on my grills (2).

Consider snow snorkeling, for example.

Usually this time of year I have fled my environs for a sunny locale where I snorkel with a dedication and commitment usually associated with, say, work. Using a reporter's uncanny powers of observation, I can report I'm not in Florida. Nowhere near. I'm in Maryland, in deepening snow, my mood teetering on some threshold best left unexamined.

I need to snorkel.

I need to pry my feet into circulation-killing snorkel fins. I need to snap on a mask that will pinch and suffocate my face. I need to suck on the puckered end of an actual snorkel and be reunited not only with ancient traces of my saliva—but with an actual hobby.

With all revolutionary ideas, however, come a few hiccups. Walking on land in flippers is tricky enough, but flopping around in the snow in webbed rubber feet is mega-humbling. Underwater agility is quickly replaced with above-ground hard labor. For those who battle recurring foggy-mask issues, snow snorkeling is not for you. You will not see a thing before you even arrive at your snorkeling grounds.

Once you have chosen a place to explore, be warned the experience doesn't take a fun turn.

I picked a random mound of snow in my backyard, dropped to my knees and ducked my masked head into the snowy depths. No marine life was visible (to be fair, I might have just picked the wrong spot). I stayed under for as long as I could, my breathing captured and categorized in sloshy bursts through the snorkel.

Then, as if by magic, I surfaced from the ocean of snow with a thought so clear, so new, so right, that I had to write it down immediately. I flopped back inside the house, took off my snorkeling gear and found one of my trusty, overpriced Moleskine notebooks. Here's what I wrote:

"Stop writing."

Because when you find yourself pining for the sun by snorkeling in the snow—and you think Weber grills talk to each other—it's time to stop.

Or go on vacation.

Bethany, My Bethany

June 28, 2015

Are you a Bethany Beach or Ocean City person?

It was a little toasty this past week.

I walked outside the office Tuesday afternoon and my entire layer of skin peeled off then drove away in my car without the rest of me (it's tricky going back to work without your epidermis—hard to get anything done not to mention the stares).

Not that I blame my skin, but how was I supposed to drive home? Would my skin tamper with my radio channels?

After a few hours, I began to worry. After all, I'm not heartless. Somewhere out there in the heat my epidermis could by lying on the side of the road, tanned beyond recognition. Not to mention out there Tuesday night in those vicious storms.

Finally, I got a text:

Hey buddy. At the beach. Dig your Sirius.

At the beach! I knew it.

And I knew what beach.

See, some us are Ocean City people, and some of us are Bethany Beach people—and some of us are Rehoboth Beach people, but I don't know any of them, so let's leave them out of this.

My better half, rather my outer half, clearly was at Bethany Beach because that's how we both roll beach-wise. The second I see Chief Little Owl, the great sculpture marking the gateway to downtown Bethany, I know I'm home away from home:

The bantam Boardwalk, biking Atlantic Avenue, walking.

Bottlenose Atlantic dolphins and ghost crabs.

World War II watch towers.

Sunset wine hours.

The smallness and quietness of it all.

Even the Sea Colony.

Even the parking hassles.

But mainly this one restaurant that serves conch fritters, Cuban pork and mojitos big enough to quench Chief Little Owl's thirst. I'd name this Bethany Beach restaurant, but that would be a blatant endorsement and violation of my journalistic code of conduct. That said, if you contact me at my top secret email address (rhiaasen@capgaznews.com) I might spell out the restaurant's name using arm gestures a la Village People's Y-M-C-A. And that's tough to do in an email. (If you want to tell me why Ocean City is better Bethany Beach, please use this address: youarewrong@nooffense.com).

So, you coming to the beach or not? I kind of missing having you around.

Oh sure, now my runaway epidermis was trying to butter me up. I texted back:

I'm kind of enjoying my summer without you. Good luck trying to swim without me.

The truth is ever since my skin left, I haven't wanted to leave the house much less look in the mirror and much less go to Bethany Beach without a protective outer layer of skin.

It wouldn't be the same.

How could I walk on the beach? Who would I sing Mungo Jerry's "In the Summertime" to? Or lament T. S. Eliot's singing mermaids with? What exactly would I apply sun block to?

And when, after staying too long out in the sun, I become a human slug capable of raising only my wine-lifting right hand, what will walk me off the best beach lest I am swept out during high tide?

I texted my better outer self:

OK, I'll meet you at Bethany. Same place?

It kept me hanging for an hour. Finally:

Same place. I'll order us the conch fritters and a Mojito. Oh, and what more thing.

Yes?

Don't forget the sun block. I'm frying out here.

[12]

Hometown Favorites

First Person: 'Cloudy with a chance of meatballs'

April 28. 2013

Let me start in the neighborhood of the beginning.

I'm the assistant editor for news at *The Capital*. In the past few months, I have snuck columns into this space. Then came a column picture and name—all of which sort of requires me to keep writing columns every other Sunday.

But here's the self-inflicted curse of writing: everywhere writers look or land, there is better writing.

I'll prove it.

This past week I ran away from work in search of 1. a public waterfront; 2. a grilled cheese sandwich; 3. the chance of running into a dog or two; 4. the chance to find a quiet seat or bench to contemplate the wonders of water, grilled cheese sandwiches and dogs. I ran away to Eastport.

I avoid knowing exactly where I'm going because nothing can be as uninspiring and soul-sucking than knowing where you will end up by car, foot or day dream. So, I happened to end up parking on First Street, walking along Jeremy's Way to a long green limb of a park, fenced on both sides, duel-dogged on one side (their barking eventually cooled). I sat on a big-backed bench overlooking the bay. It was inexcusably cold, and the water was too choppy for kayaks. There I sat, cold and choppy.

And here, new reader, is where you have to suspend disbelief because my hand, magically, felt under the rim of the bench and there, a trap door lead to a journal called "Jeremy's Way Garden Journal." I opened the water-logged, spring-green journal and eavesdropped.

"Life's demands, society's demands, have kept me from sitting in beautiful places and being filled up... I will be quiet and sit in beautiful places more often for this is what makes me "full"..."

"Ahh...the moment of peace and quiet—my 19-month-old son is finally asleep in his stroller after a busy afternoon of exploring in Eastport—our new home of almost a year."

"Ode to the slug directly underneath my feet (almost killed it)... Oh, why did you move so close to me? Can't you see I am trying to read?"

"Cloudy with a chance of meatballs."

"I think I just like seeing my own handwriting."

"The only difference between a flower and a weed is the judgment."

"Eastport rocks."

The bench and journal are signature furniture of the TKF Foundation, a nonprofit that works with groups to create urban green space. TKF has other benches throughout Annapolis with other journals for those happening upon "these sacred places." In Eastport, the bench keeps company with flower beds now heaped in mulch and a barrel of flowers as the lawn's centerpiece.

The tethered journal houses testimonials from children on their days off. People have come here after the death of a mother. People have come here on Father's Day. Other children have left drawings of sailboats, dogs, mermaids and a badminton game with accompanying text: "Why don't we play badminton anymore?"

Well, why not?

"This is my first time here but quickly it has become my favorite corner in the world."

"I want the world to know how happy I am."

All those days spoken for. And one more day, the last entry of the journal.

"Good morning, love. I can't wait for forever with you."

Volunteer caretaker tends to Brewer Hill Cemetery

May 23, 2013

She rakes dead grass off the grave with the three names and one inscription: *Forever in Our Hearts.* The woman in work gloves and white sun hat picks up the grass and stuffs her plastic bag full for another trip to the ravine down the hill.

She'll be back this week with her John Deere riding mower to navigate through the buttercupped rows at Brewer Hill Cemetery, the city's historic African-American burial ground.

Linda Simms, one of the cemetery's volunteer caretakers, doesn't plan to be buried here. But until then, way until then, the retired postal worker patrols the tilted, crumbling gravestones, raking dead grass so her mowing will come easier.

If you're in this block of West Street this Memorial Day weekend, notice Brewer Hill. The cemetery will have been mowed, and American flags will have been posted at the graves of African-American veterans from the Spanish-American War, both world wars, and Vietnam and beyond.

Credit members of the Brewer Hill Association, a group working toward the preservation and restoration of the 4.5-acre site. And credit Annapolis native Linda Simms for the mowing. She feels at home here—as much as anyone can in a cemetery.

She usually works alone, except when her trimming, raking or mowing is interrupted by deer or fox. "There's a family of foxes that come out from the ravine. They watch me, I watch them, then they watch me."

She usually works alone, except when she's interrupted by a reporter setting foot at Brewer Hill for the first time.

At first glance, the cemetery resembles a green mouth full of chipped teeth. Tombstones have fallen down; others list; still others have been seized by the soft earth. Many are homemade, with names written by hand in cement.

Cinder blocks are used to mark some graves. Here, slaves and their descendents were buried. Poor families and workers, too (cooks are buried here along with their frying pans). Not just the underclass, though. Black property and business owners are also entombed at Brewer Hill.

Notice the names: Mrs. Lottie McNeil, Florence Tongue, Hattie Jones, Adele Queen Isaacs, Crawford McPherson, Wiley H. Bates, and, more recently, civic activist Joseph "Zastrow" Simms.

Brewer Hill also honors the ugliest chapter in local race relations. "Annapolis and Anne Arundel County were given a black eye last night by the lynching of the Negro Davis," *The Evening Capital* wrote in 1906. Along the cemetery's fence, there's a plaque in the name of Henry Davis.

John Snowden, the last man hanged in Annapolis, is also buried at Brewer Hill.

It's only natural to compare the cemetery with its neighbors. Across West Street is well-kept St. Mary's Cemetery. Adjacent to Brewer Hill is the Annapolis National Cemetery, with its formations of uniform white tombstones.

"We're not regimented like that," says Simms, pulling a weed from off a marker. "We're more casual."

Many of the lot owners at Brewer Hill are long gone. Time (the cemetery was founded in 1863) and gravity (ageless) have conspired to unseat, bury and topple some of the markers.

"The ground is soft, which doesn't help matters," says Simms.

The association's work wasn't made easier after an Annapolis tour horse in 2006 broke free and spent 10 hours on the lam in the cemetery. Horse trainers tried apples and and carrots, but they didn't work.

Eventually, Princess walked into her trailer, but not before trampling the ground and damaging a tombstone. (The city's horse wrangling skills were called into question.)

There hasn't been a horse here since—mainly just the foxes that watch Simms watch them.

When you meet a person weed-whacking around tombstones, questions happen.

"Are you walking on graves? Yes, more than likely you are," she says, picking off one.

How does she mow through these broken rows?

"Oh, I don't try."

Just mows around things the best she can.

Will she buried here?

Nope. Plans to be cremated.

Linda Simms walks back up the hill to the marker with the three names. The violet artificial flowers have been bleached of color.

"I got to bring them up some new flowers," the caretaker says.

Bring who new flowers?

"My father, grandfather and grandmother."

They're buried at her feet.

First Person: My house of cards

August 11, 2013

I have wonderful news. I'm planning on buying a piece of vacant waterfront property in Eastport in an area called Horn Point. Then and there, I will build my dream home.

I know I'm a very fortunate man. Horn Point is a beautiful area were most people, frankly, can't afford to live. I feel squeamish about my good fortune, so I want to share at least some of it with you.

All of you are invited to my new home for a cookout, probably in the spring. I'll be thinking of some dates. Just let me know what you'll be able to bring. Adult beverages will be covered.

I'm getting ahead of myself. Let me tell you about the property. The land overlooks the bay with a view of sailboats, osprey nests, the Bay Bridge on a clear day and tankers every day. At least once a week I walk by my future home. Until I own it, though, I have to stay on the sidewalk and do my mental trespassing.

Once built, my home will have an outdoor dock (because docking a boat indoors is really tricky), a wrap-around porch, a single hammock and two Adirondack chairs. Indoors, I'll have the usual stuff: plumbing, electricity, doors, walls. Most of my time will be spent outside, whittling newspaper stories from driftwood, naming cocktails after bay marine life, and enjoying my new slick commute.

I live outside the county. My commute to *The Capital* is two and a half hours round-trip. Once I move to Horn Point, my commute will be 20 minutes. You can't put a price tag on that—although I will, and it will be a whopper.

Now that I'm thinking more about it, maybe early summer would be a good time for the cookout. Maybe the last weekend in June? Again, just let me know what you can bring. Thinking we'll need hamburger and hot dog buns.

One snag did emerge this week. Apparently not everyone is excited about my news. Certain "facts" have been presented to me:

1. The lot sold for $1.4 million in 2011.
2. Someone—not you—bought it.
3. Someone—not you—might build a home there.
4. You will never be able to afford waterfront property in Eastport.
5. Are you out of your mind?
6. You still live outside the county.
7. Your commute is still two and a half hours.
8. Your commute will never be 20 minutes.
9. Walking up and down the sidewalk ogling a vacant lot is not a healthy use of your time.
10. Psychologists probably have a name for this behavior.

Well, isn't that the cutest little fact parade you ever did see? And now, my rebuttal:

1. True.
2. True.
3. True.
4. True.
5. I don't understand the question.
6. True.
7. True
8. True
9. True
10. True.

That said, I'm now thinking of having our cookout July Fourth to see the great fireworks. Burgers and dogs on the grill. Drinks on me.

We'll just have to stay on the sidewalk.

'I have not yet begun to shave'

December 1, 2013

Finally, I can do something a midshipman can do.

For most of November, U.S. Naval Academy midshipmen are permitted to grow a mustache to promote men's health issues. It's the first "No-Shave November" in Naval Academy history.

Now, I've always known I am not and will never be academy material for several reasons:

1. The shearing of my hair.
2. Waking up very early against my will.
3. Waking up very early against my will to perform physically and mentally demanding exercises that do not involve having a leisurely breakfast and perhaps going back to sleep for 20 minutes.
4. Math and science.
5. Getting stepped on while trying to climb that greasy Herndon Monument.
6. Remembering to say "Sir, yes, sir" and not "Aye Aye Captain" or, even worse, "Chips Ahoy."
7. Surviving day one.
8. Surviving every day.

I've had to come to peace with something about myself. I'm a civilian. A civilian weenie.

I sweat just watching midshipmen "jog" through downtown Annapolis at a pace I categorize as Olympic sprinting.

A productive morning for me is finding two matching black dress socks for work. I couldn't bear putting any more pressure on my dress code.

And the academy's distinguished noon formation? I'd probably sleep through it. I miss my teeth cleanings, and I plan *them* six months in advance.

But I can grow a mustache, sir, yes, sir.

Just like midshipmen Eric Viscardi, James Mackovjak and Bray Wilcock, who were pictured with Alex Jackson's story in *The Capital* on Tuesday. It was Wilcock's idea to ask the academy leadership to approve the facial hair exercise. Wilcock, a man after my own heart, admittedly is not sporting a robust mustache. Depending on the sun's angle and intensity, one can theoretically detect a hair formation on the young man's upper lip.

Takes me back to my early civilian life when I attempted many a 'stache. Given my Nordic roots, the genetic deck was stacked against me (unlike a kid named Jeff I knew who was shaving at 14 months. I think he was Greek).

I was more stealthy. I often went three, four months before anyone noticed my facial hair, and then it was usually my mom, which defeated some unclear purpose. I'd like to think I just didn't want to spring my mannish growth too soon on anyone. It wouldn't have been fair to the women folk.

The only thing more imperceptible than my mustache was my beard. I once spent two years on one beard. I shaved it off—although "shaving" is too strident a verb—after my beard was mistaken for human crabgrass. This can hurt a boy.

But I'm a man now. Not to brag, but if I wanted to dedicate, say, 2014, to a beard, I could grow one within the calendar year. And I can grow a mustache with no sweat. Because finally I can do something a midshipman can do.

If only for a month.

Zip lines, oysters

November 19, 2017

Forget any Ferris wheel, Mr. Mayor-elect.

I want a zip line in the new year—one connecting St. Anne's to the State House to the Naval Academy chapel. If this route is deemed impractical or demented, I will settle for a zip line from any area outside the historic downtown that will deliver me car-less to City Dock. There, I shall install murals until I'm brought before secret circles of Annapolitans and Tasered into civic submission.

I want to install an Earle-cam. It's become apparent my Labrador spends much of his day sleeping in my bed when I'm at work. Need visual confirmation. Also, I suspect Earle has been playing our piano—and not well. Visual confirmation also required.

I want to differentiate salinity in an order of a dozen raw oysters. Fortified with this knowledge, I will make flawless recommendations to friends. They will like me more.

I want to avoid scheduling a colonoscopy one day after the Super Bowl, which was inexplicably done nine years ago. The two events are intensely incompatible. Rookie mistake. (My, how the time flies between colonoscopies!)

I want my Miami Dolphins to disband. Not permanently but for a few years. Give them time to get new coaches, new players, new team colors, new logo, new skills, stuff like that.

I want my box turtle to return to my backyard. No questions asked.

I want the next season of "Stranger Things" to be a tad less monster-y.

I want to see if I can go a year without eating meat. Meat and I have been very close over the years. Cooking meat on my Weber kettle grill is my only hobby. But maybe I could abstain for a year. I'm not talking about fish and certainly not oysters. Or shrimp. Or Hershey's

Symphony bars. Or wine—which has nothing to do with vegetarianism but also needed to be said.

I want Tom Hanks to play Captain Stubing in a movie version of "Love Boat." There is no reason for this.

I want our old spring break back, Mr. Governor.

I want to immaculately pronounce Navy coach Ken *Niumatalolo* and drop his awesome name in conversation as I order raw oysters of saline perfection.

I want to write one-sixth as well as Joan Didion.

I want to *really* understand fractions.

I want to avoid a mall this holiday season at all costs to convenience and desire.

I want to believe I've treated women with respect in the workplace and in any place, and that my words and actions—regardless of intent—have not bothered or harmed.

I want to believe when I'm wrong or stupid, I know and say so.

I want to take a walk but not alone this time.

I want that zip line.

Capital News Quiz: 8 teachable moments

November 15, 2015

What hasn't been tossed at midshipmen? And other crucial questions.

Time to dust off a shop-worn idea in the dreamy hope of rekindling readers' passions for the written word. Or, aiming lower, please take our news quiz!

Normally, we don't punctuate our ideas with cheap exclamation marks, but this will be the best news quiz ever!

Pencils ready? (Can't find a pencil? Bic pen. And not a green one. Never trusted green Bic pens.)

Red Bic pen ready?

Good.

Go:

1. What HASN'T been tossed at midshipmen as they walk to Navy-Marine Corps Memorial Stadium for football games?

   A. Snickers.

   B. Starbursts.

   C. Beer.

   D. Hamburgers.

   E. Crab cakes.

2. County Executive Steve Schuh, responding to a student's email to him regarding teacher salaries, wrote the high school senior:

   A. "Don't be another adorably naive kid who contacts elected officials and parrots something some adult told you to say."

   B. "Don't be another dumb kid who contacts elected officials and parrots something some adult told you to say."

C. "Don't be another below-average kid, who doesn't hold a master's degree in education, who embarrasses himself, his family, our great county and our great nation by listening to other adults."

D. "Let us now, mercifully, turn our attention to much more pressing issues."

3. The controversial Crystal Spring development is in what city planning and zoning stage?

A. Repeat the question.

B. Please repeat the question.

C. I don't understand the question.

D. Please don't ask me this.

E. All of the above.

4. Ginger Cove resident Es Miller turned 109 on Saturday. When Gov. Larry Hogan asked about her secret to longevity, she replied:

A. "Keep breathing!"

B. "Keep reading *The Capital!*"

C. "Keep reminding myself I'm like the coolest woman ever if I do say so myself—and I'm talking to you, too, Angelina Jolie."

D. "Keep beating Army!"

5. What is Tootie Fruiti?

A. Correctly-spelled Little Richard hit.

B. Correctly-spelled yogurt shop on Main Street.

C. Correctly-spelled staff favorite "Pet for Adoption" at SPCA.

6. Which object is NOT under consideration for Historic Annapolis' "99 Objects" exhibit?

A. $2 bill printed by Jonas Green and Anne Catharine Green from 1770.

B. Jonas Green's newly-found romance novel (with pictures) from 1772.

C. WANN microphone used by Hoppy Adams.

D. Historic murals from Carvel Hall.

7. A special zoning rule would enable the growing, processing and dispensing of medical marijuana in Anne Arundel under what circumstances?

A. Every fifth Friday between 9-9:15 a.m. in an undisclosed duck blind on the Eastern Shore.

B. Monday-Sunday, all hours, but in Amsterdam.

C. Only during County Council meetings—the really long ones.

D. Only in areas 1,000 feet from homes, schools, parks and churches.

8. A misunderstanding at a Millersville restaurant over veterans denied a free breakfast inspired what teachable moment?

A. When in doubt, give a vet his free bacon bagel sandwich and move on.

B. When in doubt, never deny anyone Starbursts or Snickers.

C. Facebook is the devil's sandbox.

Now put down your red Bic pen and see your score:
Answers: 1, E; 2, B; 3, E; 4, A; 5, C; 6, B; 7, D; 8, A

Stopping by Lafayette Park on a Snowy Afternoon

March 9, 2014

Whose park this is I think I know
The homes rich in dock and show
No one will see me stopping here
To watch this park fill up with snow.
My little camera must think it queer
To stop without a skiff or pup near
Between the benches and frozen cove
The whitest pier of the year.
I give my grandfather's coat a shake
To ask if there was some mistake
The only other sound's the sweep
Of snow splashed across the lake.
The park is lovely, light and deep
But I have relationships to keep
And miles to go before spring
And miles to go before spring.

Anne Arundel County welcomes us—with strings attached

May 3, 2016

What county slogan would you write?

The letters are back, welcoming us to our county from adjoining Prince George's County across the Patuxent River on Route 50:

Welcome to Anne Arundel County. The Best Place to Live, Work and Start A Business in Maryland.

The five, bricked county gateway signs have been under repair but are coming back online and in view of motorists. *Capital* readers called us when the letters went missing, concerned that perhaps something mysterious or even sinister was afoot. No, it's just the first maintenance done on the signs in a decade.

Still.

While it's assuring to officially be welcomed back, what's with the slogan?

We know the slogan appears on the county's website next to the picture of County Executive Steve Schuh—it's been his slogan and goal since his 2014 campaign. It's very business-friendly, family-friendly and living-friendly. But we were hoping for something more playful.

It feels like a lot of pressure, work and responsibility to live up to that action-packed slogan.

And what's with the upper caps?

Start A Business? We Get It—The Sign Oozes Pro-Business Vibes From Its Every Brick.

What if we don't want to start a business or even A Business? What if we just want to sit and have ice cream at City Dock or throw the ball around in any backyard or drive across the Bay Bridge twice in one afternoon just to look at the water?

Welcome to Anne Arundel County. The Best Place to Wander, Loaf, and Dream of Owning A Boat.

Put that on your next sign, county sign people.

Vote for me and get cool free stuff!

June 22, 2014

I believe it was Abe Lincoln who said, "You can fool all of the people some of the time, and some of the people all of the time, but you can never fool Mary Todd Lincoln especially when she's not feeling tops."

I often think of his immortal words when I'm facing life's toughest challenges.

With two days left before Maryland's primary, I am formally announcing my write-in candidacy. The question was what office would best tap into my imperceptible political instincts? What office would help me serve the most people in the least amount of time and guarantee me Fridays off?

Apparently there's already a governor's race underway. And something like 154,000 other candidates are running in the other 8,000 races (my numbers might be off, but I'm a poetry nerd not a math stud). The point is I can't compete in these other races.

Therefore, not only I am writing in my candidacy, I'm writing in a new office: president of Maryland.

After letting the grandeur of that idea cloak you in goodness, you are probably asking yourself why vote for me Tuesday.

That's a fair question.

It's also a vicious, hateful question. One of the reasons I got into politics (as of this week) was to put an end to these personal attacks. Friends warned me my personal life would no longer be personal, but I didn't think the attacks would be so ugly so soon.

But if there's anything I've learned from a life spent in politics (as of this week), is that I have a tough skin. Not tough like the skin on people's feet who work on their feet all day. Ever seen *those* feet? Whoa, man, that's some tough skin. But I'm getting off track here. Back to your hateful question.

Why vote for me?

Free ice cream.

Nothing cheers up a state or U.S. territory more than free ice cream.

Free HBO.

"Veep." Say no more.

Free paint-by-numbers redistricting maps.

Color in your very own district! If you change your mind, no problem. Just pick another color. Not contiguous? Contiguous-schmiguous! (Campaign note: Rolling out tomorrow will be my "Contiguous-schmiguous! Vote Hiaasen!" election buttons and road signs.)

Free snow globes.

Just because.

Free drizzle.

I've been hearing a lot of talk about the "rain tax" and how politicians either love it or hate it, put quotation marks around it or don't. If I become president of Maryland, I will veto or not any effort by the General Assembly to impose a tax on drizzle or even a "light mist."

My dear citizens, don't think I'm trying to buy your vote by offering you cool free stuff. I am. But governing also means having to make the hard choices. I personally won't be making those, but I pledge to hire people who not only will but live for that stuff.

Finally, a word about Tuesday's primary. Voter turnout will be staggering—maybe even in the double digits. You have something like 154,000 candidates to choose from. All I ask is that you consider me, Rob Hiaasen, for president of Maryland.

Thank you and God bless the contiguous United States of America.

Thank you, Stephen Colbert

February 14, 2016

An unlikely connection made in Annapolis

Learning to love the bomb.

Last summer, there was an avalanche of press about Stephen Colbert taking over as host of "The Late Show." In a profile for *GQ*, he talked about the plane crash on Sept. 11, 1974 that took his father's and two older brother's lives along with 70 others.

The Eastern Airlines flight carrying them went down in a foggy North Carolina cornfield due to pilot error. The NTSB found the flight crew engaged in unnecessary and "impertinent" conversation during approach (the crew talked about politics and used cars). The accident spurred the "Sterile Cockpit Rule," an FAA regulation requiring pilots to refrain from non-essential activities during critical phases of flight.

Perhaps a distant consolation for a younger brother.

"You've got to learn to love the bomb," Colbert told *GQ*. "Boy, did I have a bomb go off when I was 10."

Learning to love the bomb might have informed his comedy—performances fueled by improvisation where loss can be converted into humor. But deconstructing comedy or tragedy is like holding water in a nervous hand; it slips through your fingers and evaporates before it hits the ground. I don't *know* how Colbert came to accept and even experience gratitude for his loss. It *feels* like an impossible spiritual leap.

"It's that I love the thing that I most wish had not happened," he said. "It doesn't mean you want it."

Other interviews where he mentioned the subject included the fact his father and brothers are buried in the Annapolis National Cemetery.

Annapolis, of all places.

I went to the cemetery late last year, went there twice. I am among those drawn to cemeteries, to gingerly step among their rows, to eavesdrop on their living histories. It's not out of sense of morbidity but out of a sense of an inexplicable comfort and connection. OK, maybe it is a bit morbid.

The groomed cemetery off West Street—one of 14 President Lincoln established to keep Civil War casualties—is lined with uniform small markers honoring veterans from a cross-section of wars. In a section toward the back of the cemetery, a large, relatively new memorial towers over the other grave sites. The inscription reads: "Colbert." You can't miss if you're looking for it.

There lies the comedian's father (James Colbert, a U.S. Army veteran) and his two sons lost when Eastern Airlines Flight 212 went down as pilots chatted about used cars: Peter, 18; Paul, 15. Their mother, Lorna Colbert, was laid to rest here in 2013.

It's a curious, uneasy thing to want to visit another family's grave site. I've yet to see Colbert's "Late Show" since I don't stay up late, but I've seen where his family members are buried. It's a personal invasion of a public person. It's none of my business. I didn't want to visit, but I did. Twice.

And I read everything I could on this moment in the life of a man I feel distantly connected to.

"What punishments of God are not gifts?" Stephen Colbert also said about his loss.

Forty years ago this week, a bomb went off. My father didn't die in a plane crash. He died in our family room, marking the birth of a new normal and family narrative. He was 50.

A gift of punishment, a bomb to love.

Annapolis noir, baby.

August 25, 2013

"Try to leave out the part that readers tend to skip."
- Elmore Leonard,
from "10 Tips on Writing"
Long live Dutch.

Elmore Leonard died last week. He was 87 and was at work on his 46th novel. That's roughly a book every other year if he had started writing straight from the womb, which I don't put past him.

Leonard, who preferred the name Dutch, was the pulp minimalistic master of the dumb crook genre from "Get Shorty" and "Freaky Deaky" to "Out of Sight" and "Rum Punch." His lightning-rod dialogue lit up the page and showed readers—and reminded writers—that dialogue *is* action.

Stories abound this week on Leonard, including encore appearances of his tips for writers and his punchy first book lines. (One of my favorites: "He could not get used to going to the girl's apartment"— from "52 Pick-Up.")

His passing has rekindled my loyalty to another writer of the art of dark fiction. Someone closer to home.

A Marylander, James M. Cain was born in 1892 to parents who lived in the Paca-Carroll House on the campus of St. John's in Annapolis. (His father taught there.) Young Cain skipped a few grades and landed at Washington College in Chestertown at age 14. He later taught for a while, but his heart wasn't in it.

Some years later—and this warms my heart—Cain became a newspaper man. He worked for *The Baltimore Sun* and became lifelong friends with H.L. Mencken. But newspaper pay, then and now, can be tough pull for the ambitious, talented, lucky or all three.

Cain went west to Hollywood and made weekly fortunes hacking for the studios. When he wasn't writing screenplays, he wrote novels.

In the 1930s, Cain produced a trilogy of mysteries that remain an unparalleled string of noir classics. His characters were prone to great violence, great sex and great demise.

Allow me to tick off The Big Three:

"The Postman Always Rings Twice."

"Double Indemnity."

"Mildred Pierce."

And the stars of those movies:

Lana Turner.

Barbara Stanwyck.

Joan Crawford.

Allow me a moment to think about Lana Turner's Cora in "Postman."

You don't read "Postman"—you feel it in your bones.

The violence is essentially off-camera, but not the tension, the momentum, the attraction between Frank Chambers, the drifter who stumbles into the Twin Oaks Tavern, and Cora, the Greek's twitchy wife. They plot to kill the Greek so they can start a life together, so they can be free. They scheme to make it look like a car accident. The plan works, until it doesn't.

"Frank."

"Yes?"

"There's just one thing. We've got to be in love. If we love each other, then nothing matters."

"Well, do we?"

"I'll be the first one to say it. I love you, Frank."

"I love you, Cora."

"Kiss me."

They are doomed. It's only fair. They're killers. But we are in their pockets until the end. Just like I've been with them from the cable dramas in my life—"Dexter," "Boardwalk Empire," "Breaking Bad."

Dexter Morgan. Nucky Thompson. Walter White.

Frank and Cora.

Breaking bad until they're broken and leaving us wanting more.

Update: Athena is home

February 24, 2018

Editor's note: Shortly after our column appeared, we heard from Jennifer Brianas and her family. Athena, having left home for two weeks, appeared Sunday, Feb. 11. "She just showed up at the front door," Jennifer wrote us. (Athena and her brother, Achilles, had been gifts for Jennifer's twin daughters for their 7th birthday.) The family wanted to give a shout-out to the nonprofit Dogs Finding Dogs, a group that helps people track and find their lost pets.

Athena, dear one, get your tale back to your Annapolis home.

I don't know you or the people you live with. Hell, I don't particularly even like cats.

But here's the thing. Well, a few things.

First, leveled at me have been longstanding accusations that I'm a romantic and sentimentalist (guilty, guilty). So what if I can't pass a missing cat/but mainly missing dog poster and not blink? So what if I always stop in my tracks and spin stories for missing cats but mainly dogs?

Haven't we all gone missing at one time or another? Kind of in our DNA this urge to be unkenneled, yes.

Word on the Annapolis street (Southgate, Thompson, etc.) is you've been missing since the end of January. By the looks of your wanted poster, I imagine you are lounging and looking just like that somewhere right now. You appear wholly ignorant and unaffected by the early year's ugly news.

Did you just need to get away and chill? A misunderstanding on the homefront? Tired of the same cat food?

I like to imagine you busted out during last week's warm burst, but you skipped home well before then. Please tell us you stayed warm and away from traffic. But how would we know?

No one knows the mind of a cat; no sense in trying, either. It's like trying to figure out why none of our flashlights work. It's actually nothing like that, but it's hard to think straight when thinking about cats. They'll do that to you.

Athena—goddess of war and wisdom, subject of the final good Who song—get your tale home.

Because we need a warm splinter of good news in these gun-riddled days. I don't have any answers much less the right questions, so the path of least emotional resistance can beckon: A tiny win on the horizon. A safe homecoming.

Of course, a missing cat is nothing like those Broward County students dead and wounded or that fallen police officer in Prince George's County.

A missing cat is just a missing cat.

Until our hearts and minds, in shutdown mode, take a brief recess from watching, absorbing and feeling. Then, there, a missing cat sign on a stapled telephone pole on a neighborhood street. There, a sweet-faced distraction lounging, missing.

So, Athena, dearest one, get your tale home.

No questions, recriminations or judgment from us. If you've gained a pound of two while you were away, no worries. If you met some kind kids or other cool cats, good for you.

Just come home to tell us your story.

Peekaboo, where are you Ronald Reagan?

June 8, 2014

Annapolis is known for its funky chicken sculptures, but they're so Main Street.

Go off-road and you'll find, for one thing, one smiling, waving statue of Ronald Reagan. While not the most statesmanlike locale, Ronnie overlooks a crunched parking lot off Cathedral Street. Here he stands, the Great Communicator, his right hand extended, that smile, that John Wayne vibe.

I thought he was taller.

Still, here he stands, under an awning, protected from the sun, outside the nondescript backdoor of Maryland's nondescript GOPheadquarters. In Maryland, it's hard standing out as a Republican statue. The office had been on West Street, then moved across Cathedral Street, and now it's at Cathedral and Franklin streets.

"Every time we move, he moves with us," says Marcia Jicka, office manager at the GOP headquarters. "He's just part of the family."

She calls him Ronnie. They've been together for about four years. He used to scare the life out of her when he was stationed in the front window when they were on West Street. It's just a statue, she'd tell herself when coming to work.

The life-sized statue—with decorative pedestal—was a gift from former Maryland GOP chairman and state senator Alex Mooney, who just won a congressional primary in West Virginia. Probably would have been a hard thing to pack.

Ronnie belongs to Annapolis, where he has become a bit of a tourist attraction.

Folks stop by to have their pictures taken with him. But like other works of public art, Ronnie has been the target of hijinks. They had to chain him by his foot to the back porch so people —- "probably kids," Jicka guesses—don't tip him like a cow (apparently, there was a Ronnie-tipping incident). Someone put a cigarette in his mouth. On a more festive and healthy note, Ronnie has been sporting beads from the St. Patrick's Day celebration.

Ronnie is also a beacon for people trying to find the place.

"We tell folks to look for Ronnie in the parking lot," Jicka says.

It works.

This global bust and statuary collection in Ronald Reagan's honor is extensive. As we speak, Amazon is offering a 6-inch bust of Ronnie for about $24—"The Perfect Father's Day Gift." The full-body likeness of our 40th president (tied for eighth tallest president at a smidge over 6'1) can be seen from Warsaw to London to the United States Capitol Rotunda to, of all places, Louisiana. At a roadside attraction there in Covington, visitors can gaze up at a 10-foot bronze statue of Reagan— "The World's Largest Ronald Reagan Statue!"

I'm not sure where life ultimately takes us, but I'm guessing life won't lead me to Covington, La.

But we have our own Ronnie statue right here. He might not be the world's largest, but he's ours.

Now if only he can stay put.

Cuddle up and I'll tell you a story

August 23, 2015

Cuddle up, dove—for a price

Yet again, I've let a business opportunity slip through my writer-weak fingers.

A couple in Linthicum wants to open a cuddle business and charge people on the half hour or hour to cuddle on a bed or couch in their office. Predictably, the proposal has attracted skepticism by the less-enlightened. Some people—and they know who they are—question the very nature, the very essence, of the cuddling act in a professional setting.

"It's just a cuddle," as Tiffany Andrews told *The Capital*.

Exactly!

The entrepreneurs have spelled out a required dress code (tank tops and gyms shorts are acceptable) and tabled plans to offer overnight cuddling services. Yet, we have become such a suspicious society that some of us don't trust the simple act of paying $60 for an hour of daytime cuddling in the privacy of our own tank tops and gym shorts.

"For some cuddling positions, a pillow may be placed between a client and a staff member," *The Capital* also reported last week.

How many cuddle businesses go to such lengths to offer a buffer pillow? Now that's thoughtful cuddling.

But, as with any bold idea, questions arise.

Will spooning be offered?

When and if Tiffany and Rob Andrews hire their four staff cuddlers, will clients have their choice based on a cuddling audition?

Given Tiffany said she would have used such a service during her husband's military deployments, will military personnel be offered a discount rate?

How in the world do you get any man to cuddle for an hour?

You don't—unless you pay him.

Here is something else I know. This cuddling service would be a tough sell on the homefront. Imagine a husband and wife, first thing in the morning, discussing her cuddling appointment at some imaginary cuddling business:

Him: *"I'm deploying for the office, honey."*

Her: *"What time will you be home, darling?"*

"Usual time, my sweet significant other. What time is your cuddling?"

"The usual time."

"Frank again?"

"No, Frank broke his hip getting out of the shower. I have a replacement cuddler."

"Another old guy, eh?"

"No, a college kid. He's a lifeguard at Ocean City."

"Well, sweet darling love, I'm 100 percent OK with you cuddling with a young lifeguard."

"Two of them, turns out. They're running some kind of special today."

"Still 100 percent OK."

"And that's why I love you without even a hint of regret or need for excessive alcohol most nights."

"Wait—did you say two lifeguards?"

"Let's not dwell on such pesky details. Before you deploy for the office, my eternal soul mate, can you leave me your VISA?"

Despite any potential misunderstandings or legal separations, a cuddling business should still be given the same commercial chance and consideration as any endeavor that brings strangers together in a business setting where staff members undergo background criminal checks.

My only question is what happens *after* the cuddling.

Would I have to talk? Could I turn on *SportsCenter*? Would quality post-cuddle snacks be available?

And I'm not saying this is even remotely possible, but what if I'm not a good cuddler?

I mean, come on, an hour?

Maryland, My Maryland

February 19, 2017

What do you love about Marylander? Come on, share it.

I moved to Maryland in 1993 for a job. That's what happens. You move for a job. A job or a girl or guy.

I never moved for a girl although that is exactly something I would have done. Because no one ever will ask you years later to tell them the story of how you moved for a job. People want to hear how you moved for a girl.

So, I'm going to lie and say I moved here for a girl—a girl named Maryland.

I didn't know a thing about her before I came 24 years ago. Generally, I knew where she lived—a few states up along the coast and with some funky, alluring geography. I heard she liked crab cakes, the O's and Berger Cookies. I thought to bring her some, but I had my family to pack up. No room left in the mini-van.

First impressions:

Not quite a Southern state, not quite Northern.

Where were *good* grits?

No grapefruit trees. Had I made a perilous life decision?

First week on the job someone asked me if I was going to send my kids to private or public school. It felt like a test. It felt like no one's business.

First week on the job someone asked if I was going to join the union. My second test.

First summer I needed, severely, to see a beach lest I emotionally detonate. I rented us a place at Bethany Beach right after school let out in June. It was cold and foggy. Actual fog. We couldn't see each other, and we couldn't get into the water. I would have ingested more alcohol but the kids were very young and I didn't want them to see Daddy have to experience a Maryland jail.

First year I truly discovered John Waters, Anne Tyler, Barry Levinson, Taylor Branch, Tom Horton, Blaze Starr's old 2 O'Clock Club and my favorite noir writer, James Cain, who was from Annapolis.

Discovered homesickness fades but not completely.

Second impressions:

Canada geese.

Forget the Gators. Go Terps.

Go in-state University of Maryland tuition. Twice.

Maryland politicians appear steadfast, reasonable, moderate and unburdened by charisma.

The Unsinkable Natty Boh.

Discovered the outdoor crab tanks at "Cantler's Riverside Inn" and the *Stanley Norman* skipjack and the bewitching Maritime Republic of Eastport.

Discovered housing prices in Eastport. Bought an MRE decal instead.

Discovered *The Capital.*

Learned to take the family to Bethany Beach in August. Learned Bethany Beach isn't in Maryland.

Lasting impressions:

Home.

The schools.

The best airport.

The best sunflower field (Jarrettsville Pike and Hess Road in Baltimore County).

The best State House in any state.

Buck Showalter. I never understand a thing he says, but I sure do like the way he says it.

Veep.

The Blue Angels make me jump every time—jump out of my car, office, home and skin just to watch them.

Maryland's quick-draw fall and spring.

Old Bay.

And Berger Cookies.

Because the truth is I moved to Maryland not for a job or a girl but for Berger Cookies.

[13]

Pets—But Mostly Earle

How to find your spirit animal

June 8, 2018

Dear Spirit Animal Wrangler,

It seems everyone but me has a spirit animal. All my friends have either wolves, dolphins, owls, butterflies, tigers, horses, turtles, hawks or dragons. One friend's spirit animal is the dung beetle. He's got a bunch of other issues, so we don't ask about it. The point is they all seem extra-happy and extra-spiritual.

My questions are, how do I get a spirit animal. Are they expensive? How do I know which one is right for me?

Signed,

Wanting

Dear Wanting,

Thank you for your fake letter. Without fake letters, these columns could not exist.

Research tells us the spirit animal concept originates from animistic and totemistic beliefs—meanings of which escape us. No doubt cultural appropriation is involved. On the brighter side, internet quizzes abound to match you with a spirit animal to guide, protect, console and get good parking spaces for you. All you have to do is answer a few simple questions.

What is your astrological sign? What is your favorite color? Food? What is your favorite palindrome? Favorite skin blemish? Quiz over! Your answers will point you to your perfect spirit animal. Conversely, spirit animals take internet quizzes designed to steer them *away* from spirit humans.

Rental costs

Spirit animals can be pricey. Take your standard 100-pound Arctic wolf (not house trained). One will run you about $1,500 a month, but they do come with a cool "Spirit Animal" red bandanna. A dolphin is crazy expensive—you don't want to know.

For the more budget conscious, a standard Maryland groundhog will set you back $50 a month. Know that they under perform as spirit animals on account they tend to snuffle off and have zero interest in your spirit.

But Spirit Animal Wrangler, you ask, I need a spirit animal today for two hours tops. It's a spiritual emergency!

You're in luck, friend. A spirit animal isn't available on such short notice, but have you considered a spirit organism? We know people who know people who can get you a spirit aphid for dirt cheap.

Pros and cons

Spirit animals are widely popular because they reflect our inner lives and desires while nourishing our sense of identify through symbolism, mysticism and a lot of shedding. But they can't help you with everything.

There may or may not have been a girl in high school who wanted to "just be friends." A Shamanistic negotiation ensued.

"Could I be your spirit animal instead?"

Following a firm no, we didn't hear of her until a Facebook post 41 years later. We didn't spot any spirit animal, but her husband looks like a decent guy.

Earle, spirit animal

An alternative to searching the animal kingdom for your spirit animal is to look no farther than your backyard or bed or under bed (in the event of thunderstorms). There, our spirit animal hangs out. Earle didn't come from an internet quiz but from a lab rescue outfit. He cost about $200 for a lifetime.

Earle is neither animistic nor totemistic. He nuzzles more than guides, hides more than protects.

He's our spirit shedder.

Sami and Bella officially respond

July 12, 2016

Last Sunday I wrote about my dog Earle, a Labrador with a genetic fondness for eating—and eating.

A *Capital* reader calling himself "Old Bill" felt compelled to share the column with his Labradors, Sami and Bella.

"They were not impressed," he said. "On behalf of them and likely channeling the other two who since passed on (Fred and Wilma), I'm writing so that their viewpoints are covered."

If nothing else, we're all about viewpoints.

So, proceed Old Bill.

"Years ago with Fred and Wilma, we determined that Labs simply do not have a gas gauge—at least one that says FULL. We learned long ago that we had to watch for them.

"This was not at all appreciated by them or by Sami and Bella now. Each likes a good chew on a shoe, so we must hide them well with kiddie gates. Anyway, all of them knew the refrigerator held great delights and that must be guarded as well.

"Sami and Bella will eat anything they see. They delight in Cheerios with bananas in the morning. Sami likes hers stuffed in a Kong toy with peanut butter smeared on it. Bella likes hers in a bowl with some lactose-free milk and peanut butter.

"We've yet to start taking Sami and Bella to the trash collection station, but Fred and Wilma loved the smell from a cracked car window in mid-summer and wanted to roll in the liquids on the pavement and elsewhere. This was not allowed. Ever.

"Sami and Bella do not get to lay on the bed and watch TV with me like the others did. They do get to lay on the sofa in the 'wife cage' with her and watch TV. None of them ever had breath the couldn't knock flies off a pile of fresh dung.

"Anyway, Sami and Bella wanted to ensure that we always admire them for what they do well besides eating: Guarding the premises. Supervising the lawn care. Watching folks labor around them. That's hard work.

"Which is why they need so many naps. But there's always room for Jell-O—which they love with whipped cream!"

We are impressed, Old Bill. Thanks for writing us about your Labs. Now what is this so-called wife cage you speak of?

Earle & I: An intimate conversation

July 6, 2016

Your chubby Labrador can't help himself—blame genetics

Researchers studying 310 Labradors found that many of them were missing all or part of a gene known as POMC, which is known to regulate appetite in some species...Without it, the dogs don't know when they've had enough, so they just keep eating and eating. The New York Times

Earle:

Thank you, *New York Times.* Thank you, thank you. Maybe now a certain someone, who likes seeing his byline a little too much, will stop monitoring everything I eat every second of the day.

Me:

I saw you eat a paper bag.

Earle:

So what? I saw you eat nine oatmeal chocolate chip cookies, the ones with butterscotch in them.

Me:

I saw you try and eat my hammer. And portions of my back deck.

Earle:

That wasn't me. That was Sally, your first Labrador.

Me:

Oh, sorry.

Earle:

You can't even tell us apart. I never ate your hammer or back deck. I ate those slippers you liked so much, the ones with the tasty leathery laces.

Me:

They weren't slippers. They were sandals.

Earle:

Whatever. That were tasty.

Me:

Please explain something to me. How come when I sometimes forget I fed you and then feed you again, you don't stop and say, "No thank you, I've eaten already"?

Earle:

I'm missing part of a gene known to regulate appetite in some species.

Me:

Did you make that up?

Earle:

No, sir. Read it in the *Times.*

Me:

So, does this alleged missing gene account for your indiscriminate ingestion of Disney-esque woodland creatures?

Earle:

You just love to hear yourself write, don't you?

Me:

Don't deflect.

Earle:

So sue me, I've gobbled up a twitching chipmunk, deer hooves, maybe ducked into the compost pile a time or two, chiseled a flattened toad off the driveway here and there (note to dog self: lay off the flattened toads).

Me:

This accounts for your breath on some days.

Earle:

What's wrong with my breath?

Me:

It's missing the minty-fresh gene known to regulate foulness in most species.

Earle:

You really want to go there with me? You're not exactly Mr. Minty-Fresh Breath in the morning, pal.

Me:

Look at us. Criticizing and attacking each other. What's happening to us?

Earle:

I don't know, I don't know.

Me:

Let's just take a nice walk together. We don't have to say anything.

Earle:

Can I eat my dinner first?

Me:

You just ate.

Earle:

No, I didn't. That was yesterday.

Me:

Are you sure? I could swear I just fed you.

Highway (Dog) Philosophy

April 29, 2015

It's the age-old question:

What does a dog running down the highway have to do with anything?

Zen masters, Greek philosophers, American presidents, assorted Kardashians, have all tackled the mystery . Everyone has failed .

Until today.

The dog, a German Shepherd, was seen this week running down the middle lane of Interstate 695 on the day, the worst day of Baltimore's damaging week. Trailing the dog were police cars, and trailing the police cars were ordinary cars, many of them, slowed or stopped because of the runaway dog.

This was on the outer loop. On the inner loop, motorists — crawling in afternoon rush hour anyway — had the chance to observe the highway dog. Some took bad cell phone pictures and posted them (see above or sideways or wherever my bad picture is). At first, I thought the dog was running away from the rioting. Then I remembered dogs generally avoid civil unrest, unless they are enlisted to serve and protect, which luckily hasn't happened.

No, this was just a dog running for a mile or more down the interstate belting Baltimore. More of a casual trot, actually, with an apparent police motorcade escorting the dog. The dog was safe, for the time being.

And it made me stop and think. Not about the work day in Annapolis, but about how the unusual, the unexpected, the peaceful, the dangerous, can run us right off the road.

First Person: Earle: 6, Chipmunk: 0

July 7, 2013

About this time last year, I wrote about adopting a black Labrador named Earle. So many people responded to the column I had to shut down comments after two. Given the avalanche of interest, an update is long overdue.

My dog is a damn cat.

I'm not prone to outbursts of such profanity, but I believe those kindly Lab rescue people duped me. To the naive eye, Earle looks like the most handsome specimen of black Labrador that ever trotted off Noah's Ark. But don't be fooled like I was last year.

Earle is a damn cat.

OK, I'll stop cursing, but I've been misled. Here are the facts.

I have a backyard.

I have an electric dog fence.

I don't know how to use the electric dog fence.

Earle roams my yard, which doesn't have a fence electric, wind-powered or otherwise.

I have chipmunks.

Earle kills them.

According to one of my lazier Google searches, the U.S. dog community often opines on why dogs track the standard eastern chipmunk or "chippies," as they're called when not dangling lifelessly from the jaws of *Canis lupis*. The collective explanation for these attacks goes something like this:

Dogs are natural born hunters. Chipmunks are natural born prey. A furry appetizer darts by—maybe smirking as it does—and what are dogs supposed to do? Instinct demands action. Instinct demands the dog wipe that smirk right off that chipmunk's mouth.

I get that. Me, I'm a card-carrying member of instinct. Whenever I hear the words, "Did you call about the septic tank?," I instinctively recoil and lie.

But here's what doesn't make sense in the doggie-eat-chippie scenario. Your average dog shouldn't be fast enough to catch a chipmunk, which, while not the Mensa of mammals, certainly is a speedy varmint. Chipmunk hunting is more a cat's speed.

Except for Earle.

The second a chipmunk leaves his burrow to visit a co-ed burrow, Earle pounces. He's got the fastest first move to the hoop since James Worthy (if *one* reader gets that reference to the former Tar Heel and L.A. Laker great, I can retire a mildly happy writer.) Once pinned, the chipmunk has two choices: play dead or play alive. Both options lack hope.

Earle releases the chipmunk. It flees. Earle pounces again. Then using what experts call his "mouth," Earle chomps-then-releases the chipmunk, which is no longer smirking or moving.

At this point in nature's ballet, I get the shovel and hurl. Six chipmunks have been dispatched so far. Each time, Earle looks forlorn as he watches the crude burial ritual. Each time, my yard is diminished. Here, the box turtle, fox, deer, hawk and bat live in peace—why not the chippie?

Because I have a killer cat of a dog who plays Whac-A-Mole in my unfenced back yard.

There have been other issues.

Like when my mother-in-law visited last fall and made some sudden move and Earle nipped her in an area usually reserved for sitting. Feelings and flanks were hurt. A subsequent inquiry, complete with witness testimony, failed to establish blame in the incident.

I chose not to publicly take sides.

Call it instinct.

Earle: Just the Facts

August 26, 2012

Let me tell you about Earle.

I'm going to give you just the facts, because I don't buy into the whole dog thing. You know, *the whole dog thing.* When people talk about and sell a million books about and tell all their friends about how their dog changed their life and how their dog is the bestest dog in the whole wide world. They even use made-up words such as bestest.

Anyway, I don't buy all that, so here are the facts about Earle, who is a dog. That's fact one. Here are more facts in order of their most factfullness, a word I get to make up because I'm talking about dogs.

Earle is a black Labrador, a breed not related in any way to a full, half or quarter pit bull breed.

Earle is inherently chill.

Earle is also a chocolate Lab judging by his mocha-colored nostrils and Gorilla-like eyes. Because I'm a trained journalist, I learned when these types of Labs date seriously, the result is often a black Lab because the chocolate Lab gene is recessive, a genetic term meaning "weak or inferior to a black Lab."

Earle was rescued from a kill shelter. "Kill shelter" sounds rather inhospitable, so Earle became of special interest when dog searching began in earnest this month.

Earle appears relieved to have left the kill shelter on his terms.

Earle is 18 months old. Or 2. Or maybe a spry 6.

Earle was the name he came with. It's a noble word meaning, "that which is better named for a black Lab than a yellow."

Earle will answer to his name every single time except the times I call him.

Earle came house-trained. And this is the greatest miracle recorded since the dawn of miracles and houses.

Earle, one might concede, looks mighty cute when he balls up on the nice white sofa under the cloak of night, and no one has the desire to evict him. I'm not saying he looks cute—I'm just reporting the fact.

Earle does not appear to possess vocal cords capable of what animal experts call "barking."

Earle will never have to pay estimated taxes.

Earle, a Labrador Retriever, has been seen retrieving a tennis ball. Twice. Then, the mysteries and vagaries of Earle's mind lead him to the nearest tree.

Earle may or may not look mighty cute when he clumsily sits. Too much torso to really stick the landing. He starts sliding.

Earle replaces two family Labradors, although I've learned "replace" is emotionally inaccurate and potentially marginalizes the memory of Sally and Oscar, who may or may not have been the greatest dogs since the dawn of dogs.

Earle does not replace Sally and Oscar.

Earle is a rescue dog, who sits all clumsy, retrieves to distraction, favors white sofa fabric, won't or can't bark, might be 2 or 6 years old and embraces the miraculous value of outdoor plumbing.

Earle is our new dog.

Tail of the confused dog

April 27, 2014

Dear Maybell,

I read about you in *The Capital* last Tuesday. Every week we run pictures and blurbs about dogs or cats up for adoption at the SPCA, and your picture and story caught my eye.

But I don't want to lead you on. I already have a dog, and I'm not looking to adopt another one. Seriously. So, please consider this just a friendly note from one dog lover to one dog.

So, you're a Cane Corso mix. I'm not familiar with this breed, but no matter. You certainly have a strong, handsome face if you don't mind me saying so (I'd like to think we live in an age where a girl dog can be called handsome). The shelter folks say you have a docked tail.

I'm not a fan of the docked tail look. It's like seeing an old man in a Speedo walking slow and stooped on a beach. I'm not sure why that analogy came to mind, but I am sure I should apologize for it.

To broaden my knowledge of questionable elective canine surgeries, I researched tail docking. After seven minutes on the Interwebs, I still don't see the point of amputating part of a dog's tail.

As for you Maybell, I have questions if you can spare a little time, and it sounds like you have nothing but time these days.

1. Did you consent to having your tail docked?
2. Did you put anything in writing?
3. Was your tail so naturally long it dragged on the ground and got dirty all the time?
4. Are you a hunting dog and someone thought you'd hurt your tail in the underbrush? (I don't think you hunt. I think you're just a dog.)
5. Did someone think this would cosmetically enhance your

appearance?

6. Did the procedure hurt? Come on, you don't always have to be so tough. You can tell me how much it hurt.

OK, I'll drop it. But I wanted you to know I'm sorry your tail was docked. If I could, I'd put it back for you. Have you inquired about prosthetic tails? Probably not in your budget, I'm guessing.

Clearly your personality wasn't docked.

"Maybell is a very sweet girl," your bio says. "She gets excited when she first sees people but calms down quickly and is very well behaved."

A fine quality in a dog: initially excited, then a quick calming. No sense in overdoing the excitement, which, as we know, can lead to attempted docking of another misguided sort.

By far my favorite biographical morsel is what the shelter folks say about you trying to learn basic commands.

"Sometimes she gets confused and just lies down."

Maybell, I could kiss you for that because that's exactly what I do. Seriously. I also have trouble with basic commands. I'll be at home (or work, which is trickier) and something will confuse me and treat or no treat, down I go.

But like I said, I can't adopt you.

Still, I hope someone will take you home. Someone who is anti-tail docking. Someone who will earn your excitement and calm. And someone who will completely understand when you get confused and need to lie down.

The fine, fine brain of a cat

November 23, 2014

Ever hungry for knowledge, I opened my newspaper the other day to read our "Ask a Vet" feature and saw the following headline:

"Why is cat urinating on bed?"

Which is an astounding and relevant question for the times in which we live. The question is a parable. A metaphor. A metaphor and a parable. A metapable, if you will.

Or maybe the question means exactly what it says:

Why is cat urinating on bed?

There are cat-specific clinical and behavioral reasons for this event in the life of a cat owner. (Disclaimer: I don't own a cat because cats are inferior pets. I am, however, an inferior columnist who needed a column idea this week, so here we are.)

But I have my theories as to why a cat strays from the litter box. And while vets might say you shouldn't take it personally, you should take it very personally. It's your bed, for God's sake.

To solve the riddle of such behavior, join me as I question the brain of a cat. The interview will be brief since there is so little terrain to explore:

Cat: *What kind of crack was that?*

Me: *What crack?*

Cat: *You know what crack. The "so little terrain to explore" crack. Like cats have small brains or something.*

Me: *Don't take it personally. Like people aren't supposed to take it personally when you urinate in their beds. Let's talk about that, shall we?*

Cat: *Listen, I'm not proud of it. But it happens sometimes when, you know, I get distressed about stuff.*

Me: *What stuff does a cat get distressed over?*

Cat: *ISIS, Ebola, Jerusalem, and have you seen pics of Bruce Jenner lately? I mean, come on, how scary is Bruce Jenner?*

277

Me: *Not scary enough to forget to use the litter box.*

Cat: *Speak for yourself. Also, I take exception to the words "litter box." As if we cats, by biological association, are litter.*

Me: *What would you prefer? A decorative tray of granulated, clump-resistant, clay-based materials for personal feline use?*

Cat: *That has a nicer ring to it, yes.*

Me: *Fine.*

Cat: *Fine.*

Me: *I just said it was fine.*

Cat: *Glad you think it's fine.*

Me: *So, back to the issue. Are you telling me you have never used your owner's bed as your personal decorate tray just out of spite?*

Cat: *Why would I ever spite my owner?*

Me: *I don't know. You tell me.*

Cat: *I love my owner—even though he recently bought a very big and expensive New Yorker book of dog cartoons.*

Me: *And how did you feel about that?*

Cat: *It's fine.*

Me: *Fine?*

Cat: *Fine. That's what I said.*

Me: *Fine.*

Cat: *Like I said, I love my owner—even though he recently bought a 2015 wall calendar that features Labradors.*

Me: *And how did you feel about that?*

Cat: *Fine.*

Me: *Fine.*

Cat: *So, what else do you want to ask me?*

Me: *Where do you sleep every night?*

Cat: *In my cat bed, of course.*

Me: *Has your owner seen pics of Bruce Jenner?*

Cat: *I don't know, Why?*

Me: *Hide your bed immediately.*

Sick as a parrot? Not exactly

January 14, 2018

Sick as a dog.
Sick as a parrot.
Sick as a horse.
Sick as a baby.
Discuss.

When I get sick, I turn to whining, applesauce, bendy straws and idioms for comfort. And the internet. What follows is leached from websites I waded through despite my stomach flu, which was neither stomach-confined or the flu.

Sick as a dog.

But why a dog? How did dogs get dragged into this comparison?

The phrase apparently dates from 1705, when dogs were not domesticated house pets so much as they were ye olde wild animals. Dogs weren't given much vet care if any—none of that fancy flea and tick stuff for them. Coupled with their ancestral habit of eating anything not locked down by gravity, a dog's sickly reputation was born and co-opted to describe humans "under the weather." If I may digress—which is the most mental work I've managed this week—"under the weather" should also be banned. As I took to my bed, I took to calling my illness "euthanize me now." (The weather was never a factor.)

At my side *wasn't* my dog. Earle, sensing his owner's inner turmoil and outer whimpering, kept his distance through the gastrointestinal extravaganza. Also, I've seen him sick and, frankly, it's never been that bad. I've never said, "Wow, Earle, you look sick as a dog." Typically, I query him on what he ate, and the exchange is reduced to a very unpleasant show-and-tell.

Sick as a parrot.

OK, this is outstanding (cue: Monty Python's immortal dead parrot sketch). "Sick as a parrot" sounds so weirdly fantastic, and I had no idea what it meant.

To avoid U.S. livestock importing restrictions, sneaky people started sneaking parrots from South America into the country in the 1970s. To make sure the birds kept quiet, their carriers got them drunk on tequila as the border approached. A sleeping parrot rouses no suspicions and certainly voices no objections to elicit international travel. So, was I sick as a parrot?

I wasn't drinking tequila. I would be proposing to you now if I had been. And you'd be in the awkward position of having to decline my wedding invitation on account of we don't know each other and, oh, I'm married.

I wasn't crossing the border. I went out to a restaurant, came home, got in my quality adult jammies, and spent the next two days wishing my parents had opted against a fourth child.

I was not sick as a parrot.

Sick as a horse.

One problem. Horses can't vomit, so count me out. Don't ask me why they can't vomit or whether this is true. I don't care. The point is I *wish* I was sick as a dog or parrot or horse.

Sick as a baby.

End of discussion.

[14]

Put Down the Tequila

Put down the Tequila and step away slowly

September 7, 2014

Monster.com, a global employment website, has published an article called "Nine Things Never to Say to Your Boss." Here are the nine things, with accompanying commentary by a non-Monster.

1. "I need a raise."

"I need a raise" is rarely met with, "Please name your price and may I offer you a cool beverage while I send the appropriate emails to ensure your raise takes effect immediately."

An exception:

If you nefariously come into possession of payroll information and discover the guy next to you makes more than you, you can attempt to politely extort or otherwise shame your employer into giving you a raise. This could work.

There's a more likely outcome.

"He's worth it. You're not. Now bring me a cool beverage. Chop, chop."

2. "That just isn't possible."

Bosses never warm to such pessimism—particularly in the face of absolute reality.

Preferred responses:

"Not only is this task possible, it insults all other tasks with its vast possibilities."

"Did I say 'not possible'? I meant possible. I'm Mr. Possible!"

"I find your request refreshingly possible."

3. "I can't stand working with —."

Although justified, it's best not to share this with your boss especially if his/her name fits in the long dash longing to complete the sentence.

Here's a tip.

Flip it.

"I love working with —. I'm IN love with —. I can't get any work done around—because I'm so in love. Help me. Please."

At best, your boss will change your seat. At worst, you'll be spending much more time at home.

4. "I partied too hard last night—I'm so hung over!"

It was Tequila, wasn't it? Well, that's not important.

What's important is that you never, ever tell your boss you're hung over. Tell colleagues who might cover for you (like helping you sit upright at your desk), but don't tell your boss.

The guy who inexplicably makes more money than you? Do not tell him.

5. "But I emailed you about that last week."

Your boss gets hundreds of emails a week, of which he cares about 7. Do not assume you are in his Special Email Club for Special People.

Follow up your crucial email with a Starbucks gift card or any lawn mowing or leaf blowing needs his yard might incur.

6. "It's not my fault."

I don't have a problem with this.

7. "I don't know."

Although more acceptable than "I don't know, dude," bosses frown on naked admissions of ignorance. Plus, it's a conversation stopper. Where do you go from "I don't know"?

I don't know.

See? The vicious cycle continues.

Bosses prefer this response:

"I don't know, *but I'll find out.*"

This step regrettably leads to more work.

8. "But we've always done it this way."

You might think this is valuable perspective, but bosses tend to hear:

"But we've always done it this way. *You know, before you came and changed everything that worked. And now we're supposed to think this way is better. Excuse me while I seek Tequila.*"

Preferred response: "I don't know, but I'll find out."

9. "Let me set you up with..."

That's just weird.

Sober and reporting for duty

July 27, 2014

I'm an imposter.

Let me explain, but first are you sitting down? Savoring your first or second cup of Sunday morning coffee?

It's addictive, isn't it? You need it. Gives you that antsy rush, your sweet little caffeine addiction that you love and cherish and is named in your will.

But what if someone told you the coffee you've been drinking for years has been *decaf?*

Your life, your mood, your decisions have all been a ruse. Your stained teeth and obsessive coffee ritual and mood swings have been for naught.

Still enjoying your coffee?

Still think it's caffeinated?

You better check, dear ones.

I've reportedly been drinking decaffeinated coffee at work. I say "reportedly" because that's the word journalists use to hedge their reporting in the face of unbelievably horrific news.

A colleague innocently pointed out to me that the drum of coffee I've been shoveling from is neutered coffee. I received the news with the level of excitement and anticipation I felt when non-alcoholic beers were introduced. A part of my soul died.

I slowly put down my favorite coffee cup (there goes the favorite coffee cup concept) and walked slowly toward my office (what's next— someone tells me my office hasn't been real either?). Then, just as slowly, things began to make sense.

I had begun drinking more and more coffee throughout the day, losing track of how many times I filled her up. But no matter how much I consumed, I never achieved that jittery rush that could make me short-tempered with co-workers and co-loved ones until my buzz burst reducing me to a fetal position under my desk. God, I missed that feeling.

More delicately, my coffee runs also led to many daily pit-stops. I worked in fear my colleagues thought I had a bladder glitch or merely was acting my age. All that private work was for naught, too.

Day in and day out, I was just downing and drowning in one placebo after another.

Now I question all my addictions.

Is my "occasional" glass of Pinot Noir really a bootleg strain of Welch's grape juice?

Is my "Apollo 13" movie obsession based on a false premise that man really stepped foot on the moon?

Is my Charlize Theron really dating Sean Penn — he of a perfect bladder?

I don't know what is real anymore. My chemical compass has been disconnected. I find myself walking by the old coffee station, peering at the canister of decaf as it mocks me.

Maturity requires I accept this with grace and accept this as a sign I didn't need coffee in the first place. That's Maturity talking but after a couple of cups of *real* coffee.

I dare Maturity to go a day or a week or a month without real coffee at work. Let's see how mature Maturity is then.

See we just need for a few small things to go right in life because the larger things, if left to their own compass, can go wrong and break our hearts. And when this happens, you need a little comfort, a little something to go right.

Like a cup of coffee.

Love you like a brother (and other motivational workplace lines)

March 11, 2018

The pinnacle of human interaction and communication is often experienced in the workplace.

I'm not sure who said that, but it was probably the guy who promised to keep his meetings short. Truthfully, the pinnacle of human interaction and communication is nowhere to be found—except in Paris and on certain beach days.

Us bosses don't mean to utter weaselly sayings at work. Maybe our language is born of self-preserving habits, as if a giant workplace callous has formed on our souls. That's *my* idea but …

I want this to be your idea …

Or, say, the opposite of your idea.

Not to tell you what to do …

I'm going to tell you what to do. Bask in my omniscience.

Not to tell you to bask in my omniscience …

Bask. Repeat.

I know you were already thinking this …

Although when I looked into your eyes, they silently screamed: HAVE YOU BEEN DRINKING?

We're going to keep our meetings short …

Did I mention how shorter meetings have proven to be more productive and soothing to the morale of a company? I didn't? I thought I had. Meetings need to be planned, have a purpose. It's important to have plans and a purpose. It's important in a meeting to be prepared, have plans and a purpose. A meeting without preparation, plans and a purpose is an unproductive meeting. It's important a meeting is productive. And has a purpose, as long as the purpose is prepared and productive. That's really important. I told you all this in our last meeting, right?

Did you get a chance to see my email from the other day?

The one I sent three times, followed by two follow-up emails because you never check your emails or are ignoring mine.

I know you aren't ignoring my emails …

I ignore my emails.

There's no "I" in team …

So stop spelling team "teim." It looks ridiculous.

Thanks for taking the lead on this …

And for not involving me in any aspect of what you are taking the lead on. God speed, brother.

I love you like a brother …

Like Cain loved Abel?

Not to interrupt your lunch …

Stop chewing while I'm talking to you. And are you going to finish that Wawa burrito?

Just to help me remember, did you put your days off on the vacation calendar?

I know you didn't because I checked.

Did you tell me you are off Friday?

I know you didn't because I would have remembered.

You're off Friday, right?

Oh, right, I forgot you told me.

Remember we talked the other day about that (fill-in-the-blank) issue …

And we both got defensive and shut down and felt lousy for about 13 minutes and left colleagues stunned and fearful. And it wasn't the "other day"—whatever that squishiness means. The day was yesterday at 2:16 p.m., as enshrined in my weekly planner that I still haven't been reimbursed for.

What are your initial thoughts?

So we can blast by them and get to my final thoughts.

Have you given any thought to …

Law school?

Not to speak for you …

But would you stop talking so I can speak for you?

Why yes, that is a waste basket on his head

December 17, 2017

Subject: Holiday office party

From: Human Resources

To: Employees

By now many of those working at our properties are planning office holiday parties for employees.

For legal purposes: "December" is defined as any day falling within the month where employees may (or may not) observe a religious observance. "Properties" is hereby defined as a parent company owning children companies that may (or may not) be subjected to applicable bedtimes. "Party" is defined as a highly regulated, nonalcoholic, nonmusical gathering of employees at the workplace during work hours. Legally, it is not synonymous with "party."

We encourage employees to share the spirit of the holidays—provided productivity is not interrupted. Along with our unconditional support (and unwavering gratitude for keeping party costs under $50), we feel compelled to remind employees of a few common-sense tips.

For legal purposes, "common-sense tips" are iron-clad edicts. "Iron-clad edicts" are edicts that are legally clad in iron.

We want everyone to have a safe, legal and subdued office party. Toward that end, here are those few common-sense tips:

"Iron-clad edicts."

Remember, you are still at the office. True, you have gathered with colleagues in a cramped conference room to enjoy covered dishes and covered conversation while adapting to the lack of chairs. But you are still at work. And you are a professional and a valued member of our parent company—despite another year of no raises or bonuses (our gift to you is you still have a job). Please act accordingly.

"Act accordingly" is best defined by a few examples: 1. If a colleague's eye color has mysteriously changed from peckish green to spotlight blue and septum, lip, cheek and dimple piercings have appeared on his face, it is not appropriate to ask "What HAVEN'T you pierced and can we all see?" 2. If a colleague is wearing a recycling wastebasket as a decorative head ornament, it is not appropriate to dump trash on his head. 3. Sprite with tequila shots is not an acceptable workplace drink. Neither is Sprite.

It might seem like we are telling you NOT to have fun. Not true! There are many ways of having safe, legal and subdued fun as you celebrate the holidays with colleagues, some of whom you talk to once a year.

Why not a fun board game? While we cannot permit Twister ("a lawsuit waiting to happen," our lawyers have advised), what about Apples to Apples or Candy Land? In-between taking turns, folks have time to develop goals for the new year! Take turns sketching out goals on an erasable chalkboard! Turn your holiday party into a work party! We'll provide the chalkboard and two (2) Sharpies.

Where supplies are available.

In conclusion, we wish you a very merry office party.

But do you deserve a summer office party?

June 25, 2017

It's summer. It's hot.

You don't feel like working.

You deserve a break.

Blah, blah, blah.

Well, it might be time for an office party, but how can you be sure? A party is its own organism, ecosystem and universe. An office party is an organism within an organism. Its frailty is well-documented, and few if any survive an hour. It's the riskiest social event you ever will attend. Still, you might need one.

Want to be sure?

Answer these super easy questions correctly and it might be time you have an office party—at your own risk.

1. You look up from your desk and see colleagues staring blankly at:

    A. You.

    B. Their Instagram.

    C. Their fading hopes and dreams.

    D. Their fading 401(k).

    E. Any of the above.

2. The highlight of your summer work day is:

    A. Enviously watching window washers repel the side of your office building.

    B. Counting the number of gray Hondas and Toyotas in your parking lot.

    C. Deleting junk mail. Slowly.

    D. Securing an overdue appointment with your dental hygienist.

E. Any of the above.

3. Routine, reliable office features fail you:

A. Clocks have stopped or are playing cruel tricks ("How can it *still* be 9:30 am?").

B. One of two ice trays in fridge snaps in half, reducing office's ability to even form ice.

C. Office runs out of red Bics. No one cares but you. You feel very, very alone.

D. None of the above.

E. C only.

4. Your sense of time is warped:

A. You think it's Friday, but it's only Wednesday.

B. You think it's Friday, but it's only Monday.

C. You think it's Friday, but it's only Monday—two Mondays ago.

D. You think it's 2014.

E. Any of the above but mainly D.

5. OK, you decide to have an office party and discover:

A. Window washers are a hoot.

B. People never bring spare ice trays to a party.

C. Dental hygienists are way more fun when they're not sand-blasting plaque off your central incisors.

D. The "summer party" pizza tastes remarkably like the "some-one else is leaving" pizza.

E. The party seemingly lasts forever due to the broken clock.

F. You discover you actually *like* your job and co-workers.

G. All of the above.

The job evaluation selfie

January 26, 2014

What makes an occasionally above-average employee question his above-averageness?

What makes an occasionally confident employee sink to new depths of self-doubt and paranoia?

Filling out their own self-evaluation.

Much like another ritual for people of a certain age, job evaluations also require setting aside private time for uncomfortable personal probing committed by person or persons not in your immediate family.

Imagine saying what you *really* mean about your job if it didn›t mean the end of your job...

Please list your accomplishments in the past year:

Slow down, Mr. Team Leader. What exactly do you mean by "accomplishments"? Is that some dig at me for finally remembering to get my time card in on time last week? Or finally learning how to transfer calls?

Also, you refer to the "past year." Do you mean human years or dog years? The difference is whether I'm being asked to cite my accomplishments for the last year or for the last seven years—and if the latter is the case then clearly I'll need a lot more room than this dinky space.

Please clarify.

Please list the training and job skills you developed in the past year, including team skills:

In team settings, I have learned it's not productive to hurl a loaded stapler at colleagues even when they are so wrong they're practically begging to be hit by a loaded stapler.

Please list the barriers that keep you from accomplishing your individual and team goals:

1. Contact with other humans.
2. The industry standard known as the 40-hour work week.
3. Lack of summers off.
4. Cheetos that get hung up in the vending machine after I pay the dollar.
5. Lack of current sports magazines left on lunchroom book-shelf.
6. Goals.
7. Expectations.
8. Expected goals.
9. When certain area sports teams fail to meet their goals thus ruining my weekend.
10. Additional contact with humans.

These are the skills and training you feel are necessary for you to achieve your goals:

I've always wanted to play tight end in the NFL.

Please train accordingly.

Do you want to revise your performance plan for 2014? (You do.):

OK, I suppose the NFL is out of the question if the point is to crush my dreams.

Please list ways your team leader can help you improve your performance:

1. Don't crush my dreams.
2. Offer praise (both verbally and in writing) when I accomplish tasks that fall under "above and beyond." I've heard of this above and beyond stuff. Sounds suspicious and tiring.
3. Offer unjustifiable raises to me. The kind of raises that if my coworkers found out, they'd throw loaded staplers at me.
4. Renew subscription to *Sports Illustrated* in lunchroom. *Maxi-m*optional.
5. Please observe my "quiet time" between 11 a.m. and 4 p.m.

6. In the event of another polar vortex or 1-3 inches of snow, I'll be working remotely from Sloppy Joe's Bar in Key West. Call after 4 p.m. when my "noisy time" begins.
7. Discount Cheetos in vending machine!
8. Re-adjust my performance expectations to meet the talents and maturity of a 13-year-old boy.
9. When communicating detail-oriented tasks for me to perform, please speak slowly and softly. If possible, light incense and put on James Taylor to increase my comfort level. Also, think of deadlines not so much as specific points in time but as Einsteinian concepts of expanding, infinite units of so-called time. Or let's just shoot for next week.
10. Optional Attendance Fridays.

Yours in above and beyond performing,
R. Hiaasen, valued employee

People, if you read nothing else

January 25, 2015

I'm often asked to speak at Fortune 500 companies and lowly civic organizations where I share my business expertise with the less mentally fortunate.

My message is simple: Success is earned through hard work, visionary leadership, superior physical and mental strength, and a few snazzy neckties.

"But I don't work hard or possess visionary leadership or superior and mental strength, and I don't own anything snazzy. Is there a short-cut to success?" is a question I often get.

There *is* a shortcut!

It's all in the business cards.

We all know the problem with work. It's people. They're everywhere. And they want things. And they are never happy. Or grateful. They want, want, want. They talk, talk, talk.

But if you follow my strategy, you will never have to speak to another human at work!

"That sounds too good to be true!"

But it is true, Fake Person Talking in Quotations.

Say a colleague comes up to you with a perfectly reasonable question. He's a pretty good guy. You had lunch with him, once. You know the names of one of his two kids. But he's interrupted your solitude, and this will not stand. Here's the perfect business card for the occasion:

With profound regret, I don't have the information you are requesting. I do, however, appreciate your inquiry and how's (son's or daughter's name) doing?

Some people—and they know who they are—want to "follow up" with you. This is highly offensive but it happens, let's be honest. Play this business card:

I'm renewed in your question's grandeur. I'm sorry to hear (son's or daughter's name) was arrested.

Say the same colleague, undeterred, enlists your boss to help "get a simple answer out of you." It's unfortunate the relationship has deteriorated to the point, but don't panic. Just reach into your house of cards:

I'm both flattered and invigorated knowing two of my colleagues seek my input. Thank you, and best wishes for a joyous and productive work day.

Now there is a slim chance this won't work. We can all get depressed why this can happen given the generosity and professionalism contained in my business card strategy. Let's stay positive and work through this challenge together.

Say those two employees have enlisted a third employee, say, from HR. This does not stand for Home Run (which would be fun) but rather Human Resources—a fringe society of colleagues that operates by a series of secret handshakes and underground tunnels. Their questions tend to be more pointed. Again, don't panic. There's a business card for them, too.

I didn't know our building contained a window-less, darkened, sub-basement beset with boa constrictors. Thank you for inviting me to see where you work. I'm relieved to hear your (son's or daughter's name) was able to post bail.

You should be all set.

But if this fails, you can always break completely down and talk to people.

No man is an island, I know, I know.

How do you spell s-t-r-e-s-s?

January 12, 2014

The folks who broke the news that newspaper reporting was the worst job of 2013 have come out with another cheerful list. Newspaper reporters have the eighth most stressful job.

Police officers came in ninth.

That's right—according to CareerCast.com, newspaper reporters have a more stressful job than police officers. But do you know who has a more stressful job than police officers *and* reporters?

Newspaper *editors*.

Remember last Thursday when Anne Arundel county police surrounded a Glen Burnie home and eventually charged a man with building a destructive device? Remember the search lasting something like seven hours, the neighborhood block closed off, and unfounded rumors swirling that other devices could have been planted throughout the county?

That scene was nothing compared to the stress I feel any given day in the newsroom. I wish the public or the police or CareerCast.com could walk in my shoes for just one week. They don't know the meaning of stress.

Let them try to predict the preferred pizza toppings for a group of ravenous reporters working the holidays. You try and be in charge of ordering pizzas for *that* crew. There›s always going to be some rogue vegetarian requesting some unholy topping such as pineapple (why not throw battery acid on your pizza?). There will be griping about a mass order of pepperoni pizzas even though pepperoni is God's choice of topping and it says so right there in the Book of Genesis, I think.

Show of hands—how many of you have to spell every single word correctly every single time?

Granted, police officers face potential dangerous situations every day, but do they fret over spelling Truxtun Park? Do they live in abject fear of spelling it Truxton Park—or misspelling the name of Navy's head football coach? Do they suffer from the recurring nightmare of committing career-crippling typos, such as leaving the "l" out of "public"? No, they do not.

And let them—and the others with so-called more stressful jobs such as military generals and airline pilots—try and conquer our newsroom printers. Sooner or later, Satan's toys will tear your heart out and feed it to you on a pizza.

Settling staff vacations?

Settling vacation conflicts?

Settling staff conflicts?

Settling more pizza conflicts?

I'd rather land a 747 on a skinny, rocky Bahamian airstrip. During a Category 5 hurricane. With no landing gear. While nursing a tequila hangover.

I didn't mean that. I'm just stressed out. You try remembering the first name of that nice man who comes in the evening and takes the trash out of your office and you talk a little sports and thank him three times but still can't remember his name because you're a pathologically timid person.

OK, deep breaths. Deep, deep breaths.

And spell after me . . .

Ken N-i-u-m-a-t-a-l-o-l-o. . .

Please let that be right.

Benefiting Organization
The Coalition to Stop Gun Violence

At the request of Rob Hiaasen's wife, Maria, Apprentice House Press will make a contribution to The Coalition to Stop Gun Violence.

The Coalition to Stop Gun Violence seeks to secure freedom from gun violence through research, strategic engagement, and effective policy advocacy.

We are countering the gun lobby through cutting-edge policy development and aggressive advocacy. Our commitment to addressing gun violence in all its forms and advocating for at-risk individuals sets us apart.

Learn more: https://www.csgv.org